TIME AND ETERNITY

TIME AND ETERNITY

ANANDA K. COOMARASWAMY

MANOHAR
2023

First published 1903
Reprinted 2023

ISBN 978-81-19139-10-1

Published by
Ajay Kumar Jain *for*
Manohar Publishers & Distributors
4753/23 Ansari Road, Daryaganj
New Delhi 110 002

Printed and bound by CPI Group (UK) Ltd, Croydon, CRo 4YY

CONTENTS

LIST OF ABBREVIATIONS

RV = *Ṛgveda Saṁhitā;* TS = *Taittirīya Saṁhitā;* AV = *Atharvaveda Saṁhitā.* AB = *Aitareya Brāhmaṇa;* JUB = *Jaiminīya Upaniṣad Brāhmaṇa;* PB = *Pañcaviṁśa Brāhmaṇa;* ŚB = *Śatapatha Brāhmaṇa;* AĀ = *Aitareya Āraṇyaka;* ŚĀ = *Śāṅkhāyana Āraṇyaka.* U., or Up. = *Upaniṣad;* BU = *Bṛhad-āraṇyaka Up.;* CU = *Chāndogya Up.;* KU = *Kaṭha Up.;* MU = *Maitri Up.;* Kaus. = *Kauṣītaki;* Muṇḍ. = *Muṇḍaka;* Śvet. = *Śvetāśvatara;* Taitt. = *Taittirīya.* Mbh. = *Mahābhārata;* BG = *Bhagavad Gītā.* BrS = *Brahma Sūtra* (text); BrSBh. = *Brahma Sūtra Bhāṣya* (Śaṅkara). Manu = *Mānava Dharma Śāstra.*

Vin. = *Vinaya Piṭaka;* A = *Aṅguttara Nikāya;* D = *Dīgha Nikāya;* M = *Majjhima Nikāya;* S = *Saṁyutta Nikāya;* Sn = *Sutta Nipāta;* Dh = *Dhammapada;* KhP = *Khuddaka Pāṭha;* Mil. = *Milinda Pañha;* J = *Jātaka;* Vism. = *Visuddhi Magga;* Dpvs. = *Dīpavaṁsa.*

AJP = *American Journal of Philology;* BSOS = *Bulletin of the School of Oriental Studies;* JAOS = *Journal of the American Oriental Society;* JHI = *Journal of the History of Ideas;* JRAS = *Journal of the Royal Asiatic Society;* NIA = *New Indian Antiquary;* HJAS = *Harvard Journal of Asiatic Studies;* SBE = *Sacred Books of the East;* ZDMG = *Zeitschrift der Deutschen Morgenländischen Gesellschaft.*

Philo Judaeus: Gig. = *De gigantibus;* Heres = *Quis rerum divinarum heres sit;* LA = *Legum allegorium;* Opif. = *De opificio mundi;* Spec. = *De specialibus legibus.*

Evans = C. de B. Evans, *Meister Eckhart,* vols. I and II, 1924 and 1931; Pfeiffer = Fr. Pfeiffer, *Meister Eckhart,* 4th ed., 1924.

Shams-i-Tabriz: *Dīwān* = R. A. Nicholson, *The Dīwāni Shamsi Tabrīz,* 1898.

TIME AND ETERNITY

INTRODUCTION

Τὸ δὲ πρότερον καὶ ὕστερον ἐν κινήσει ἐστίν, χρόνος δὲ ταῦτ' ἐστίν ... τὰ ἀεὶ ὄντα, ᾗ ἀεὶ ὄντα, οὐκ ἔστιν ἐν χρόνῳ Aristotle *Phys.* 4. 14, 223 A + 4. 12, 221 B.

Nunc fluens facit tempus, *nunc stans* facit æternitatem, Boethius *De consol.* 5. 6.

In ēwikeit ist weder vor noch nāch ... Allez, daz got ie geschuof ... die beschepfet got nū zemāle, — Meister Eckhardt, Pfeiffer pp. 190, 207.

It was an everlasting beginning, — Jacob Boehme, *Mysterium Pansophicum* 4. 9.

In principio ... id est in verbo ... in sapientia fecit, — St. Augustine, *Confessions,* 12. 20, 28.

Anyatra bhūtāc-ca bhavyāc-ca ... anādy-anantam ... īśāno bhūta-bhavasya-ca evādya sa u svaḥ[1], — *Kaṭha Upaniṣad* 2. 14, 3. 15, 4. 13.

---

[1] Nec praeteritus nec futurus, sine initio aut fine. Dominus omnium praeteritorum et futurorum, Ille solus est hodie atque cras.

> *Οὔτε γεγονὼς οὔτε ἐσομενος, ἅτε ἄναρχος καὶ ἀτελεύτητος ὤν, ἀλλὰ κύριος ὢν πάντων τῶν γεγονότων καὶ ἐσομένων, οὗτος μόνος ἔστι σήμερον καὶ αὔριον*

Aided by Professor George Chase, and Professor Werner Jaeger, I put this into Latin and Greek only to show how easily and perfectly Latin, Greek and Sanskrit can be translated from one to the other.

"Need there is, methinks, to understand the sense in which the Scripture speaketh of Time and Eternity" (Dionysius, *De div. nom.* X. 3)[2]. Here, the doctrine of Time and Eternity will be discussed in Vedic, Buddhist, Greek, Christian, and Islamic contexts. Both terms are ambiguous. "Time" is either all or any part of the continuum of past and future duration; or that present point of time (*nunc fluens*) that always distinguishes the two durations from one another. Eternity is either, from our temporal point of view a duration without beginning or end or, as it is in itself, that unextended point of time which is Now (*nunc stans*).

From what may be called the fundamentalist or literalist point of view, time in the first sense is thought of as having had a beginning and as proceeding towards an end, and so contrasted with eternity as everlasting duration without beginning or end. The absurdity of these positions is made apparent if we ask with St. Augustine, "What was God [the Eternal] doing before he made the world?" the answer being, of course, that inasmuch as time and the world presuppose each other and in terms of "creation" are "concreated", the word "before" in such a question has no meaning whatever. Hence it is commonly argued in Christian exegesis that ἐν ἀρχῇ, *in principio*, does not imply a "beginning in time" but an origin in the First Principle; and from

[2] Cf. St. Augustine, *De ordine* 2. 51: "In this world of sense it is indeed necessary to examine carefully what time and place are, so that what delights in a part, whether of place or time, may be understood to be far less beautiful than the whole of which it is a portion".

this the logical deduction follows that God [the Eternal] is creating the world *now,* as much as he ever was.

The metaphysical doctrine simply contrasts time as a continuum with the eternity that is not in time and so cannot properly be called ever*lasting,* but coincides with the real present or now of which temporal experience is impossible. Here confusion only arises because for any consiousness functioning in terms of time and space, "now" succeeds "now" without interruption, and there seems to be an endless series of nows, collectively adding up to "time". This confusion can be eliminated if we realise that none of these nows has any duration and that, as measures, all alike are zeros, of which a "sum" is unthinkable. It is a matter of relativity; it is "we" who move, while *the* Now is unmoved, and only seems to move,—much as the sun only seems to rise and set because the earth revolves.

The problem that arises is that of the locus of "reality" (*satyam; τὸ ὄν; ens*) whether reality or being can be predicated of any "thing"[3] that exists in the flux

[3] The words "real" and "thing" have an interest of their own. "Real" is connected with Lat. *res,* and probably *reor,* "think", "estimate"; and "thing" with "think", denken. This would imply that appearances are endowed with reality and a quasi-permanence to the extent that we *name* them; and this has an intimate bearing on the nature of language itself, of which the primary application is always to concrete things, so that we must resort to negative terms (*via negativa*) when we have to speak of an ultimate reality that is not any thing. That a "thing" is an appearance to which a name is given is precisely what is implied by the Sanskrit and Pali expression *nāma-rūpa* (name, or idea, and phenomenon, or

of time and is therefore never self-same, or only of entities or an all-inclusive entity not in time and therefore always the same. A brief discussion of this problem will provide a setting for the treatment of the traditional doctrine of time and eternity.

Sanskrit *satyam* (from *as,* to "be"), like τὸ ὄν and οὐσια (from εἰμὶ, to "be"), is the "real", "true", or "good",—ens et bonum convertuntur. In these senses, *satyam* can be predicated of existents[4], for which

---

body) of which the reference is to all dimensioned objects, all the accountable individualities susceptible of statistical investigation; that which is ultimately real being, properly speaking, "nameless". "Name-and-appearance in combination with consciousness are to be found only where there are birth and age and death, or falling away and uprising, only where there is signification, interpretation, and cognition, only where there is motion involving a cognizibility as such or such" (D. 2. 63).

The Vedantic position is that all differentiation (naturation or qualification) is a matter of terminology (*vācārambhaṇaṁ vikāraḥ,* CU. 6. 1. 4-6, cf. S. 2. 67 *viññānassa ārammaṇam*); and in the same way for Plato, "the same account must be given of the nature that assumes all bodies; one cannot say of the modifications that they *are,* "for they change even while we speak of them", but only that they are "such and such", if even to say that much is permissible (*Timaeus* 50 A, B). In this passage, the "nature referred to is that primary and formless matter that can be informed,... nature as being that by which the Generator generates" (Damascene, *De fid. Orth.* 1. 18) or "by which the Father begets" (St. Thomas, *Sum. Theol.* 1. 41. 5).

[4] Throughout the present article, "exist", "existent", etc are used in the strict sense of *ex alio sistens,* and to be distinguished from "being" or "essence" *in seipso sistens.* The distinction goes back at least to Plato's opposition of γένεσις = *bhava* to οὐσία = *astitā*, survives in St. Augustine (*De Trin.*

"things" in all their variety the collective term is "name-and-shape" (*nāma-rūpe; ὁ λόγος καὶ ἡ μορφή*, Aristotle, *Met.* 8. 1. 6): and by this (relative) truth, that of the name-and-shape *by* which God is present in the world (ŚB 11. 2. 3. 4, 5), and *as* which *it* is differentiated (BU. 1. 4. 7; CU. 6. 3. 2), "the Immortal, the Spirit of Life is concealed" (*etad amṛtaṁ satyena channam; prāṇo vā amṛtaṁ, nāmarūpe satyaṁ, tābhyām ayam prāṇaś channaḥ*, BU. 1. 6. 3), just as the Sun, the Truth, is concealed by his rays (JUB. 1. 3. 6), which he is asked to dispel so that his "fairer form" may be seen (BU. 6. 15, Īśā Up. 15, 16). In the same way, the powers of the soul are "true" or "real", but "the Truth that the Self is, is the Reality of their reality, or Truth of their truth" (*satyasya satyam ... teṣām eṣa satyam*, BU. 2. 1. 20); it is "that Reality, that Self, that thou art" (CU. 6. 10. 3). In this absolute sense, also, Truth or Reality (*satyam*) is synonymous with Dharma, δικαιοσύνη, Justice, Lex Aeterna (BU. 1. 4. 14), one of His names "who alone is today today and tomorrow" (BU. 1. 5. 23): and he only who knows this Ultimate Truth (*paramārtha-satyam*) can be called a master-speaker (*ativadati*, CU. 7. 16. 7 with Comm.), "nor ever can our intellect be sated, unless *that* Truth shine upon it, beyond which no truth has range" (Dante, *Paradiso* 4. 124-126) [5].

---

6. 10. 11), and is fully dealt with by St. Thomas (*De ente et essentia*).

[5] The Vedantic and Buddhist distinction of empirical knowledge, valid for practical purposes, and prob-able, from the intellectually valid and axiomatic truth of first principles is the

It is, then, *from* the relative truth of name-and-form that the Comprehensor is liberated (*nāmarūpād vimuktaḥ*, Muṇḍ. Up. 3. 2. 8); however it may be a valid truth for practical purposes, it is a falsity or unreality (*anṛtam*) when compared with the "Truth of the truth, Truth absolutely, and it is by this falsity that our True Desires" are obscured. In other words, temporal "things" are both real and unreal. The Vedanta does not in fact, as has so often been asserted, deny an existence of temporalia,—"for the distinct suchness (*anyattattvam*) of this world of affairs, evidenced by all criteria, cannot be denied" (BrSBh. 2. 2. 31), "the nonexistence of external objects is refuted by the fact of our apprehension of them" (*nābhāva upalabdheḥ*, BrSBh. 2. 2. 28). That Śaṅkarācārya misinterprets the Buddhist position, which avoids the extremes "is" and

same as that of "opinion" from "truth" in Greek philosophy; opinion corresponding to becoming, and truth to being (Parmenides, Diogenes Laertius 9. 22, Diels frs. 1, 8; and Plato, *Timaeus* 28, 29); opinion having to do with "that which begins and perishes" and truth with "that which ever is, and does not begin"; the distinction, surviving in Leibnitz' two forms of intuition, one giving "the truth of fact", the other "the truth of reason", is virtually, and perhaps actually, a restatement of Democritus, who recognized "two forms of knowledge, respectively bastard and legitimate, the former reached by the senses, the former reached by the senses, the latter intelligible, reason being the criterion". (Sextus Empiricus, *Adv. Dogm.* 1. 138 f.). Modern "pragmatism", of course, deals only with the "bastard" truth of facts, according to which, for example, we *expect* (though we do not *know*) that the sun will rise tomorrow, and act accordingly. Hence, also, the modern concept of art as a merely *aesthetic* experience.

"is not" (S. 2. 17, cf. BG. 2. 16), is irrelevant in the present connection. The point of importance is that the Vedantic position is in perfect agreement with the Platonic, which is that things are "false" (ψεῦδος = *anṛta*) in the sense that an imitation, though it exists, is not "the real thing" of which it is an imitation; and with the Christian doctrine as formulated by St. Augustine in *Conf.* 7. 11 and 11. 4: "I beheld these others beneath Thee, and saw that they neither altogether are, nor altogether are not. An existence (*esse*) they have, because they are from Thee; and yet no existence, because they are not what Thou art. For only that really *is,* that remains unchangeably; Heaven and Earth are beautiful and good, and are (*sunt*), since God made them", but when "compared to Thee, they are neither beautiful, nor good, nor are at all" (*nec sunt*). The Vedantic doctrine that the world is "of the stuff of art" (*māyā-maya*) is not a doctrine of "illusion" but merely distinguishes the relative reality of the artefact from the greater reality of the Artificer (*māyin, nirmāṇakāra*) in whom the paradigm subsists. The world is an epiphany; and it is no one's fault but our own if we mistake "the things that were made" for the reality after which they were made, the phenomenon itself for that of which phenomena are appearances![6] Moreover, "illusion" cannot properly be predicated in an object, it can only arise in the percipient; the shadow is a shadow, whatever we make of it.

[6] Cf. Anaxagoras, "things apparent (τὰ φαινόμενα) are the vision of things unseen" (Sextus Empiricus, *Adv. Dogm.* 1. 140); and Romans 1. 20.

I

HINDUISM

In ŚĀ. 7, cf. AA. 2. 3. 5ff., a series of progenitive triads is expounded on the analogy of grammatical crasis. *Saṁdhi,* the crasis of prior and posterior forms [e.g. as Sāyaṇa says, of $a + i$], really neither confuses nor splits them apart. To pronounce in Nirbhuja fashion without distinction [as *e*] is appropriate for one who desires only food, earth (this world); to pronounce them in Pratṛṇṇa fashion separately [as *aï*] is appropriate for one who desires only the sky (yonder world); to pronounce them in Ubhayamantareṇa fashion, i.e. in the intervenient Middle Way [as *ai,* diphthong], includes both and is appropriate for one who desires both worlds, and so "the mora that declares the crasis is their harmony (*sāman*)[1], combination or union (*saṁhitā*)".

In general, the "prior form" is the mother, the "posterior form" the father, their combination or union (*saṁhitā*) the child. Analogous triads are, *in divinis,* Earth and Sky, parents of the Gale or Lightning or Time (*kāla*): or subjectively, within you, Voice and

[1] Evidently to be taken here in the sense of the hermeneia *sāman* = *sā* + *ama* "she and he", as in AB. 3. 23, JUB. 1. 53. 4, and CU. 6. 1 and 7, cf. my *Spiritual Authority and Temporal Power* ..., 51ff.

Mind, parents of the Breath, or Truth, or Knowledge, or Self; and Prescience[2] and Faith, parents of Sacrificial-Action (*karma*)[3]. But the most significant from the present point of view is the further triad, procession (*gati* = *pravṛtti*) and recession (*nivṛtti*), parents of stasis (*sthiti*). All measures of time, from *dhvaṁsi*'s up to Years, are united in this union (*saṁhitā*), that of the Stasis,—"it unites these times" (*kālān saṁdadhāti*). The text goes on: "Time (*kāla*) unites procession, recession, and stasis, and by these All This (world, or universe) is united"[4]. That is, *in divinis*. Subjectively, psychologically, "the past (*bhūtam*) is the prior and the future (*bhavyam*) the posterior form, and the present (*bhavat*)[5] is their union (*saṁhitā*), or product". In illustration of this, the Āraṇyaka quotes RV. 10. 55. 2, "Great is that hidden Name, and far extending, whereby thou madest past[6] and Future (*bhūtam ... bhavyam*)"

---

[2] *Prajñā*: Keith's mistaken and unintelligible "offspring" merely reflects the misprint *prajā* in his own edition of the text, *Aitareya Āraṇyaka*, 1909, 210.

[3] Cf. ŚB. 11. 3. 1; and AB. 7. 10 where the sacrificer represents Truth, and his wife, Faith.

[4] Essentially, this is the doctrine attributed by Rāmānuja to the Jains: " 'Time' is a particular atomic substance which is the cause of the current distinction of past, present, and future" (in comment on BrS 2. 2. 31, SBE XLVIII, 516).

[5] Note that *bhavat*, as an honorific, is also "Presence", as, e.g. Milton, "Sov'ran Presence", and cf. the doctrine of "Total Presence".

[6] Keith's "present" is an obvious slip, as he has, rightly, "past", for *bhūtam*, above.

After "hidden Name" might have been added AA. 2. 3. 8. 4 *yasmin nāmā ... tasmin devāḥ sarvayujo bhavanti* and AV. 10.

and might have cited AV. 19. 53. 5 and 54.3: "Sent forth by Time (*kāla*), what hath been and shall be

---

7. 22 [skambha = brahma] *yatrādityāś rudrāś-ca vasavaś-ca* [the *prāṇāḥ* of CU. 3. 16, elsewhere often = *devāḥ*] *samāhitāḥ*.

It may be worth noting in the present context that "the original sense of the perfect was not distinguished from the present in point of time but denotes a state" and that this "oldest sense is common in the Rgveda ... ['past'] participles which express a completed action whose results persist into the present", Keith, *Aitareya Āraṇyaka*, 1909, p. 211, n. 8 and 247, n. 1. Examples of participles are "the originally timeless force of the form *kṛtya*" (*ib*. p. 179, n. 1, cf. Whitney, *Sanskrit Grammar* 889, 894); and in RV. 1. 81. 5 *jāto*, "not impf. 'was born' or aor. 'has just been born' but 'exists, having been born' ", and BD. 8. 47 *stutāḥ*, not "were praised" but "are praised". Something of the same sort can also be recognized in that kind of ancient art in which successive events of what is verbally expressed by narrative are represented as if occurring simultaneously, in one and the same frame. Again, in Genesis, no time interval can be inferred as between "Let there be light" and "There was light", which is also the light that is now. The common Buddhist expression *yathā bhūtam*, "as become", used with reference to things "as they really *are*" implies the ripening of past causation in present effect. Some scholars assume that such forms as *he may, he can*, "are survivals of a primitive atemporal era, when 'preterites' were used indifferently for the present" (G. Bonfante in *Word* I, 1945, p. 148). "To the Hopi, time is not cut up into segments which can be measured, like an hour, a day, or a year, but it is rather conceived as a duration, in which the Law is being fulfilled" (Laura Thompson, "Logico-aesthetic Integration in Hopi Culture", *American Anthropologist* 47, 1945, p. 542): "Once we have rid our minds of the idea of parts of Time ... all the notes are held together by the uninterrupted succession which in this case is the tune" (F. H. Brabant, Time and Eternity in Christian Thought, 1937, p. 177). As I have often remarked, the "long stand apart ... Time hath engendered what hath been and shall be", and KU. 4. 13 "Lord of what hath been and shall be, He is both today and tomorrow", and AV. 10. 7. 22: "Wherein what hath been and shall be, and all worlds are instant (*prati-tiṣṭhatā*), tell me thou of that Pillar (*skambha,* Axis Mundi), what it may be".

Note, above (1), that Time is on a par with Lightning and (2) the words, "Time unites procession, recession, and stasis" (*kālo gatinivṛtti-sthitiḥ saṁdadhāti,* SA. 7. 20). This last can only mean that here Time (as in AV. 19. 53 where Time is the *source* of past and present, and so cannot be identified with either one or both of these durations) is a static *point*, that of the Stasis in which the two contrary motions *momentarily* coincide, but which otherwise separates them. The root in *sthiti* is *sthā,* to "stand", "exist", "be in a given state", implying stability, and contrasting with *gam,* or *car, cal,* to "go" or "move", implying instability: "what goes" and "what stands" together making up the whole of the existence of which the Sun is the Self (RV. 1. 115. 1). The contrast of "standing" with "going" may be noted in Mbh. 13.96. 6 where the Sun

---

ago" or "once upon a time" with which our fairytales *begin* are really timeless expressions (cf. Hebrew *olam,* rendered by Gk αἰών): and a remarkable illustration of this can be cited in the fact that the Indian fable so often begins with *asti,* "There *is*", for example, the first story in the *Pañcatantra,* beginning *asti kasmin-cit pradeśe nagaram,* "There is a city in a certain land",—a statement that is not specific as to time or place. The myth is *really* ἀεὶ γὰρ ἐν ἀρχῇ.

"stands at mid-day for half a twinkling of an eye" (in Jamadagni's words, addressed to the Sun, *madhyāhne vai nimeṣārdhaṁ tiṣṭhasi*); that is not, of course, to be thought of as a measurable period of time. For even for those who thought of the sun as daily ascending and descending, a real pause in the Zenith was always miraculous [7], and neither does the revolution of the earth, which makes the sun seem to rise and decline, ever stop [8].

---

[7] As in J. I. 58 where the sun stands still above the Bodhisatta for so long as he is plunged in *jhāna,* but still moves for others, and this is expressly a *pāṭihārya;* and Joshua 10 13 "the sun stood still in the midst of heaven".

[8] Consider a stone, thrown into the air vertically; how long does it "hang" in the air before it begins to fall again? The answer to this depends upon the fact that the vertical projection of a missile, which first rises and then falls, is only the limiting case of a course that is really curved. When a missile is projected not merely upwards but at the same time forwards, it also rises first and then falls; but its course is an unbroken curve, and we do not even imagine that it stops or hangs for however short a time at the highest point of the curve; and in the same way in the case of vertical projection there is no actual time, however short, during which it "hangs", but only a point without duration in which the upward and downward motions, past and future, *meet.*

The problem is fully dealt with by Aristotle (*Phys.* 8. 8. 262 A), who shows that when the direction of motion of a continuously moving object is reversed we cannot properly say that the object "has reached" or "has left" the point at which the reversal takes place, "but only that it 'is there *at* an instantaneous 'now' (εἶναι ἐν τῷ νῦν) and not *in* any space or period of time at all" (Wicksteed and Cornford's rendering). The point at which the reversal takes place is no more an actual stopping place than are any of the other of the indefinitely numerous

On the other hand, as in the case of the miracles cited [7], so in that of the Comprehensor, the Sun [9] "having risen in the Zenith, will no more rise nor set, but will stand (*sthātṛ*) in the middle ... For the Comprehensor of this Brahmopaniṣad, it is once-and-for-all (*sakṛt*) day" (CU. 3. 11. 1, 3) [10]. And, also, with reference to Brahma, "there is this indication: *in divinis*, That in the Lightning that flashes forth and makes one blink (*nyamīmiṣat*); and within you, That which, as it were, comes to the mind, and by which one instantly (*abhikṣṇam*) [11] remembers,—that concept (*saṁkalpa*)"

---

points on the way, in each of which the object *might* have stopped but did not.

To avoid any possible confusion, it should be realised that the final "coming to rest" of the object on the ground is not a "stasis", but only a condition of relative immobility for some period of time beginning from the terminus of the particular kind of motion first considered; though this does not arise in connection with the sun or earth, of which the motion is continuously of the same kind. In any case, "all rest is in time" (*Phys.* 4. 14, 221 B).

9 Here the "intelligible Sun",—"not the sun whom all men see, but the Sun whom not all know with the mind", AV 10. 8. 14, i. e. Apollo as distinguished from Helios, Plutarch, *Moralia* 393 D, "the Sun of the Angels" as distinguished from "the sun of sense", Dante, *Paradiso* 10. 53, 54, Philo's "Sun of the sun", *Spec.* 1. 279.

10 "Thy sun shall nevermore go down", Isaiah 60. 20; "There all is one day, series has no place; no yesterday, no tomorrow", Plotinus, *Enneads* 4. 4. 7; "the eternal day which neither dawns nor sets", St. Augustine *In Ps. CXXXVIII.* Many other parallels could be cited, e.g. ŚB. 12. 2. 2. 23, and St. Augustine, *Conf.* XI. 13. 16.

11 *Abhikṣṇam* = *abhi* (intensive) + *kṣaṇam*, see *JAOS.* 24.

(Kena Up. 4. 4, 5): on which Deussen comments, "Das zeitlose Brahman hat sein Symbol in der Natur an dem momentanen Blitze, in der Seele an dem momentanen Vorstellungsbilde" (*Sechzig Upanishad's des Vedas*, 1907, 208)[12].

11, note: or perhaps better, *abhi* + an obsolete *ikṣṇam*. Cf. *kṣaṇa-dyuti* and *nimeṣa-kṛt* = "lightning": and in the *Sāhitya Darpaṇa* 3. 3 *lokuttara-camatkāra-prāṇa*, with reference to the "tasting of Brahma". *Kṣaṇa* should also be noted as "leisure" and "festival", cf. Lat. *mora:* and also *kṣaṇa* as "*opportun*ity", i.e. *gate*way. In some uses, *ikṣ*, to "see", "eye", is precisely to "consider", in the primary sense of this word.

[12] Lightning is the standard symbol of divine manifestation, revelation and illumination, a brilliance "like lightning in that it lights up the whole body at once", MU. VII. 11; "in the Lightning, Truth", Kauṣ. Up. 4. 2. "The Person in the Lightning is the Breath, the Harmony (*sāman*), Brahma, the Immortal; as it were a sudden (*sakṛt*) flash of lightning, and even such is his splendor who is a Comprehensor thereof" (JUB. 1. 26. 8 + BU. 2. 3. 6). *Sakṛt* is "one-making", "once", "but once" (Macdonell, *Vedic Grammar* 306, 409, Keith, *Sanskrit Literature* 229): the opposite of *asakṛt*, "recurrent", MU. 2. 4.

"Suddenly a light, as if from a leaping fire, will be enkindled in the soul", Plato, *Ep.* 7; "the principle of knowledge, that is conceptual, pure, and simple, flashes through the soul like lightning and offers itself in a single moment's experience to apprehension and vision", Plutarch, *De Iside* c. 77; "the moment of (supreme) illumination is short-lived, and passes like a flash of lightning" (Eckhart, Evans. ed. I. 55); "suddenly there shone from heaven a great light", Acts 22. 6; "the Lord spake suddenly unto Moses", Numbers 12. 4. For the *Abhisamayālaṅkāra,* when the End of the Road has been reached, the Full Awakening (*abhisambodhi*) of a Buddha is "single-instantaneous" (*ekakṣaṇa-*), see E. Obermiller in *Acta Orientalia* 11. 81, 82, and Index, s. v. Cf. Zen *satori*. The event is truly "momentous". Many other parallels could be cited.

In AV. 19. 53 and 54, cited above, "Time"—absolutely—is the source of all relative times; not itself a duration, but rather the Timeless, Eternity, to which all moveable time is ever present. It is in these terms that the Maitri Upaniṣad distinguishes the "two forms" (*dve rūpe*) of Brahman, i.e. aspects of the two natures (*dvaitibhāva*)[13] of the single essence (*tad ekam*), as "time and the Timeless (*kālaś-cākālaś-ca)*: "From one who worships, thinking 'Time is Brahma' (*kālam brahmeti*), time (*kāla,* also death)[14] reflows afar. As it has been said:

From Time flow forth all beings,
From Time advance to their full growth,
And in Time, again, win home,—
'Time' is the formed (*mūrti*) and formless, both.

There are, indeed, two forms of Brahma; time, and the Timeless. That which is prior to the sun is the Timeless (*akāla*) and partless (*akala*); but that which begins with the sun is the time that has parts (*sakala*), and its form is that of the Year ... Prajāpati ... Self[15]. As it has been said:

---

[13] MU. 7. 11. 8; cf. BU. 2. 3, MU. 6. 22 etc.

[14] "Day and night are death, but they do not affect the divinity Āditya (Sol invictus), for they are only the occasion of his rising and setting" (*Vādhula Sūtra*), but really "he never rises nor sets" (AB. 3. 44), "for the Comprehensor it is evermore high noon" (CU. 3. 2. 3).

[15] The solar Self (*ātman*), transcendent and immanent, "is called time (*kāla*), who devours all existences (*bhūtāni*) as his food" (Maitri Up. 6. 2); it is from this all-devouring solar time or death that the concept of a timeless Time is a deliverance. Cf. Claudian, *Stilicho* 2. 427-430.

The time (that has parts) cooks (*pacati,* matures) all things,
In the Great Self, indeed;
But the Comprehensor of That (Time without parts) in which time itself
Is cooked, *he* knows the Vedas!

This extended (*vigraha,* specific, hypostasised) time is the regal-river of begotten beings ... (the ultimate source) of All This here, and of whatever fair or foul there is to be seen in the world" (MU. 6.14—16)[16].

"Other than 'has been' and 'shall be', without beginning or end, Lord of what has been and shall be, He alone is today and tomorrow" (KU. 2.14, 3.15, 4.13). He, then, "who is partless, the constant amongst the inconstant, the One of the many, all-maker, all-knower, immortal, omnipresent (*nityo nityānām ... eko bahūnām ... viśvakṛd viśvavit ... amṛta ... sarvago ... niṣkalam*) is the "creator of time" (*kālakālaḥ, kālakāraḥ,* Śvet. Up. 6.13—19): "at the command (*ājñā,* as a verb, primarily to know, hence to exercise authority) of that Imperishable (*akṣara,* also "Word", Logos) the moments (*nimeṣā*), hours, days, ... and years exist apart"

[16] The formless and undivided Time of MU. corresponds to the absolute Time that "unites procession, recession, and stasis" (ŚĀ. 7.20 cited above), i.e. past, future and present, and to Śaṅkara's "impartite Time" (*niṣkala kāla)* of which the aeons, years, seasons and all other "times" are only "imagined" arrangements (*kalpita, Vivekacūḍāmaṇi* 497). In other words, all duration is an articulate form imposed by our own thinking on a Reality to which all such articulation is foreign.

(*vidhṛtās tiṣṭhanti,* BU.3.8.9). And such is what William Morris rightly calls "the entering in of time from the halls of the outer heaven".

For the *Yoga Sūtra Bhāṣya* 3.52, a moment (*kṣaṇa*) is the "ultimate minimum of time, and cannot be further divided up ... and the continuous flow of such moments is their 'course' (*krama*) ... Their uninterrupted course is what is called 'time' ... The whole world passes through a mutation in any one moment; so all the external qualities of the world are relative to this present moment". The control of the moments and their sequence leads to a discriminative gnosis, of which the final development (*ibid.* 54), "the Deliverer" (*tāraka*), "has all things for its object, and all times, without-regard-to-their-course (*akrama*) as its object". It will be seen that this is the same procedure that is described in the Buddhist *Kālacakratantra* cited below; it reminds us also of Meister Eckhart's saying, "Not till the soul knows all that there is to be known, can she pass over to the unknown good".

Finally, for the Vedanta, the reality or actuality of things is only momentary; it is folly to say of the world that it "is"[17]; and "neither is 'I' a substance, since 'it' can only be seen for an instant (*kṣaṇikatvadarśanāt*); how can the words 'I am omniscient'[18] hold good for the I, etc. that exists for a moment only?" *(aham-*

---

[17] "How can that which is never in the same state *be* anything?" (*Cratylus* 439 E).

[18] "The Self knows everything", MU. 6.7. This could not be said of the inconstant, empirical self or "I".

ādeḥ kṣaṇikasya, Vivekacūḍāmaṇi 230, 293). In view of this it is difficult to follow Śaṅkara's polemic in BrSBh. 2. 2. 20 directed against the Buddnist doctrine of "instant dissolution" (*kṣaṇika-bhanga-vāda*)[19]. Śaṅkara rejects the Buddhist doctrine on the ground that it is incompatible with the operation of causality[20]; but that is an objection that would only hold good if the doctrine had been one of a discontinuous time made up of successive instants; whereas the Buddhist doctrine is that the stream of existence is incessant (*na ramati,* A. 3. 147), and carries along with it the momentum (or potential) engendered by all that has taken place in the past, and that the "individuality", however incons-

---

[19] For the Buddhist doctrine in detail see the following chapter.

[20] It seems to be from exactly the same point of view (involving a misunderstanding of the traditional doctrine) that the notion of the "instantaneous present" is rejected in "modern" theories of time; for example, by Whitehead (*The Concept of Nature,* p. 73) who insists that "past and future meet and mingle in an *ill-defined* present" [i.e. in what Buddhaghosa calls the "extended moment" (*santati-khaṇa*)]. This is to ignore that any such "ill-defined" present must consist of two parts always "with a narrow ledge of definite instantaneous present" determining them, but without interrupting their continuity because it has no duration and is not in time.

It is not in the instantaneous present, but in time and space, that causality *operates;* and it cannot be too strongly insisted that in the traditional doctrine everywhere time and space are uninterrupted continuities, and that were it otherwise the hare would never succeed in passing the tortoise. It is only when time is thought of as *dis*continuous that the operation of causality becomes unthinkable.

tant, is always the heir of past actions of which the effects mature in due course, whether sooner or later[21]

[21] This "sooner or later" is essential to a proper understanding of the concepts of "gradation" and "evolution". The traditional idea of "evolution" is "emergent". Accordingly for St. Augustine "the world is pregnant with the causes of things as yet unborn", "so that at this time or that, and in this or that way, the thing created may *emerge*... break out and be outwardly created in some way by the *unfolding* of their proper measures" (*De Trin.* 3. 9. 16); a thing or species is eternal in the Word of God "in which there is no then and sometime", but it "comes into being at that time 'when it ought to come into being'" (*De gen. ad litt.* 1. 2. 6); and "as in the seed there are invisibly and at one time all the things which in course of time will grow into a tree, so the universe must be conceived" and in this way those things which are producted by the operation of physical causes existed potentially (i.e. as possibilities) "before in the course of time they [actually] came into being in the shape in which they are now known to us in those works which 'God worketh until now', John 5. 17" (*ib.* 5. 23. 45). In other words, their preexistence as possibilities is what is meant by "gradation" while their emergence in the course of time is their "unfolding" or "evolution". The doctrine of "seminal reasons" is not unlike the theory of "genes" by which we now interpret "heredity". Further, analogous to this phylogeny is the ontogeny of individual organisms. Just as the pure Intellect embraces the ideas of many things in simultaneous identity with itself, as species are included in a genus, "so it is with the powers (δυνάμεις) in seeds (each with its corresponding matter, such as moisture); not distinguishable in the whole, the form-active-principles (λόγοι) are, as it were, all present at one point (ἐν ἑνὶ κέντρῳ). And there already are the formative-principles of the hand and the eye, which will be separately known when they come into being together with their sensible matter... This some call the 'nature in the seed' ... which, coming out

Again, the Vedantist Cakrapāṇi, commenting on the *Caraka-saṁhitā* (1.1.55, 1.8.11, 141.1)[22] admits that cognitions are momentary (*kṣaṇika*) but, he says "not as in the Buddhist scriptures 'lasting for a moment only'" (*eka-kṣaṇavasthāyinyaḥ*); for there is also a continuity (*saṁtāna*) because of which the experiencing Self[23] is called a Unity (*ekatayā ucyate*); and this Self is eternal, though the rise of consciousness in it is occasional; constant, or eternal, "because of the concurrence of its own past and future intuition" (*nityatvam cātmanaḥ pūrvaparāvasthānubhūt ārtha-pratisaṁdhanāt)*[24]. But the opposition is unreal, because the

like light from fire, and not mechanically as so many have said, moulds the matter by bestowing upon it the formative-principles... Given the formative principle, and the matter that can receive that seminal reason (*λόγος σπερματικός*), the living thing itself must come into being" (Plotinus, *Enneads* 5.9.6 and 10). "Sicut autem in ipso grano invisibiliter erant omnia simul quae per tempora in arborem surgerent", St. Th. Aquinas, *De gen. ad litt.* 5.23.45).

The Indian texts are rather less detailed; but it is very much in the same way that Uddālaka, taking for granted that "the Self (Spirit") knows everything" (Maitri Up. 6.7), expounds the nature of the Self to his son by comparing it to the infinitesimal germ that you cannot see in the seed, but will become such a great banyan tree as you see yonder (Chāndogya Up. 6.12, cf. Manu 1.56).

[22] See in Das Gupta, *History of Indian Philosophy* 2.367, 368.

[23] "Experient immanent Person" (*bhoktā puruṣo'ntasthaḥ*, Maitri Up. 6.10); "whom the wise call the experient" (*bhoktety āhur manīṣiṇaḥ*, Kaṭha Up. 3.4); "the Lord, the experient" (*bhoktā mahe'svaraḥ, Bhagavad Gītā* 13.22).

[24] All experiences or intuitions being ever present to the "one

Buddhist predication of a merely "single-moment-enduring" experience is to the transient self that is "not my Self", while the Vedantist continuity and unity is that of the true experient, at once my Self and the Self of all beings. The whole, or almost the whole basis of the Vedantist critique of Buddhism seems to rest upon the erroneous supposition that in Buddhism both the transient *and* the real selves are denied; whereas, it is clear enough from the canonical Buddhist scriptures that while the Buddha denied the reality of the transient self (of which he allowed a postulation only for every-day purposes), it can have been only of the Self—"the Lord of the self", Dh. 160, 380—that he is speaking when he "takes refuge" in it himself, and recommends others to do the same.

Reference must also be made to the Indian "atomism". The word *aṇu,* often synonymous with *sūkṣma,* "subtle" or "acute" (cf. *sūci,* "needle"), is not literally "atom", but does mean "indivisible particle or principle", so that *aṇu,* or *paramāṇu* and *aṇutva,* are

---

and only transmigrant, ... the Lord", Praśna Up. 4. 5, etc.: see my "Recollection, Indian and Platonic", Supplement No. 3 to *JAOS,* 1944.

Cakrapāṇi's formula, explaining the meaning of *nityatvam,* is an admirably concise enunciation of the doctrine that eternity is that Now to which the past and future are ever *present.* Note that *nitya* ($\sqrt{ni}$, Gk. *ἐ-νί*, "in") has also the primary meanings of "*in*nate" "native", "own"; cf. *ni-ja,* "innate", "own", and *ni-vid,* "Vorschrift", "canon", "code". Hence one might render Cakrapāṇi's formula more freely: "The intrinsic nature of the Self is its present contemporaneity with whatever has been or will be".

the real equivalents of "atom" and "atomicity", and may be translated accordingly; the related *āṇi* is the sharp "point" of anything, such as an axle or needle; and I render *aṇiman* by "minimum", though in some contexts it stands rather for the *power* to assume the "minimum" form (which is really that of the "thread-spirit", *sūtrātman*), in which alone it becomes a possibility to pass through "solid matter" or wherever there is no dimension through which to pass. Furthermore, and just as ἄτομος can be used of either spatial or temporal minima, so the reference of *aṇu* may be either to a "point" of space, without dimension, or to a "point" of time, without duration.

"Atomism" is primarily associated with the Vaiśeṣika position (*darśana*), which takes its name from the fact that the material atoms are regarded as having each its own "particular" (*viśeṣa*) eternal quality or substance. Kaṇāda's [25] avowed purpose in the *Vaiśeṣika Sūtras,* regarded by Das Gupta as pre-Buddhist, is to explain Dharma (Eternal Law) as the ground on the one hand of eventuation (*abhyudaya*) and on the other of the

---

[25] "Atom-eater", from *kana,* minutium, mote, drop, atom etc., related to *kana* as used for *alpa* in comparative and superlative forms, and present in such words as *kanyā,* young or virgin girl, and *kaninaka,* pupil of the eye, cf. Ir. *cain,* undefiled. The contents of the Sūtras is conveniently summarised by Das Gupta, *History of Indian Philosophy* I, ch. 8; but Das Gupta's own comments must be read with some reservations, e.g. where he says that for Kaṇāda Time is the ultimate cause and for this idea elsewhere refers only to Śvet. Up. 1. 1. 2, ignoring on the one hand MU. and on the other RV. 10. 55. 2 and the AV. and ŚĀ. references cited above.

Summum Bonum (*niḥśreyasam*), i.e. Liberation[26]; the validity of the Vedas is established by the fact that such are their results. Time is the cause of temporalia, but absent from eternal things. "Self" is not an inference drawn from behaviour, but directly known in the experience "I"[27]; it is one in all, but seems to be many because of the particular limitations of the things in which it is manifested[28]. Nonexistence (*asat*) is the absence of activity and quality; the four types are recognized, prior (potentiality of existence), posterior (no longer in existence), mutually exclusive (definitive, "this is a jar" implying "is not a cloth"), and absolute (antinomial, like "the horns of a hare"). Causality (*hetu*) is relation; but cause and effect have no independent existence, and because of this *yutasiddhy-abhāva* need not be thought of as either "connected" or "dis-

---

[26] Thus, as in Buddhism, both temporal and eternal, in the world and not of it. "The characteristic of the traditional solution of the space-time problem is that reality is both *in and out of* space, both *in and out of* time" (Wilbur Urban, *The Intelligible World,* p. 270).

[27] This is a proposition quite different from Descartes' Cogito ergo sum, where the argument is based on behaviour and leaves us still in an ego-centric predicament. Kaṇāda's "I" refers to what the author of the *Book of Privy Counselling* calls "the naked blind feeling of thine own being... not clad with any quality of thy being".

[28] Thus both one and many, as in ŚB. 10. 5. 2. 16; one really, and many only logically, as for the Vedānta, passim. Plato's "nature that assumes all bodies" (*Timaeus* 50 A, B); Rūmī's "one single soul that is nominally manifold in relation to bodies" (*Mathnawī,* 4. 414-8).

junct"; all production "depends on the operation of unseen causality" (*adṛṣṭakārika*), and where there is no such causal operation, there is Liberation. An atom is "an everlasting uncaused existence" (*sad akāraṇaṁ, nityam,* VS. 4. 1); the atoms themselves are spherical; atomicity (*aṇutva*) and magnitude (*mahattva*) are the basis of the concepts large and small; but both can be predicated of the same thing at the same time. Śaṅkara's rejection of the Vaiśeṣika doctrine of the elemental atoms in BrSBh. 2.2.11—17 consists essentially in a demonstration that constituent parts of things, however small, must be of some size, and can no more than aggregates be thought of as everlasting; this is undeniable, but even so would seem to leave the Vaiśeṣika system fundamentally valid if regarded strictly as a "point of view" (*darśana*), i.e. as an ontology in which the development of physical atoms is taken for granted and no attempt is made to go behind them. In any case, what must be avoided is any confusion of material "atoms" with the really atomic and partless time or space that is not a "part" of time or space in the way that material atoms are parts of things in time or space. Let us observe, in passing, that neither Sanskrit *aṇu,* "minute", nor Greek *ἄτομος,* "indivisible" (*acchedya*) [29], actually predicates an absolute lack of size. The "atoms" of modern science have been "split", and are no longer atomic, but composite, particles. We can now consider the true atomicity or homogeneity

[29] BG. 2. 24; *avibhaktaṁ ca bhūteṣu ... vibhakteṣu,* BG. 13. 16, 18. 20, cf. Clement of Alexandria *Stromata* 6. 4 "the Spirit of God indivisibly divided to all".

of the ultimate reality without further reference to Kaṇāda[30].

In RV. *aṇu* occurs only as an adjective, "fine", qualifying the "fingers" that prepare and qualify the Soma. But *āṇi* (*κέντρον*) as "axle-point" is significant in I. 35. 6 where "as upon the axle-point of the [cosmic] chariot stand fast the immortals" (*āṇiṁ na rathyam amṛtādhi tasthuḥ*)[31]: and since the "axle" here must be identified with the pneumatic Axis Mundi (RV. 10. 85. 12 *vyāno akṣaḥ*), its "point" corresponds to Dante's "punto dello stelo a cui la prima rota va dintorno ... da quel punto depende il cielo e tutta la natura" (*Paradiso* 13. 11 + 17. 17); and the proposition really answers the (perfectly intelligible) question, "How many angels can stand on the point of a needle?" Elsewhere *aṇu* stands for the "fine point" or "subtle essence" of anything, as in JUB. 3. 10. 3 where the Brāhman Kāṇḍviya is looked down upon because he "did not seek for what is atomic in the Sāman (*aṇu sāmnaḥ*), in which respect Prācīnaśāli surpassed him"; Kāṇḍviya had "missed the point". Atomicity and immensity are attributed simultaneously to the ultimate reality in

[30] For an excellent and much fuller discussion of Indian atomism, see A. B. Keith, *Indian Logic and Atomism*, Oxford, 1921. The subject is very difficult, and in so far as the question is one of material (elemental) atomicity or particularity has no very important bearing on the doctrine of time and eternity. Keith considers it possible that the Indian theory may be partly of Greek origin, but has no decided view.

[31] *Āṇiṁ na rathyam ... adhi*, i.e. *arā iva rathanābhau saṁhatā ... yatra*, Muṇḍ. Up. 2. 2. 6.

which these two, and all, extremes meet; and this implies at the same time a total and omnipresence, and the coincidence in eternity of whatever is everlasting with whatever is now,—sicut erat in principio. "Less than the atoms (*aṇubhyo'ṇu*), in whom the worlds and their inhabitants are set, that is the imperishable Brahma, Truth (*satyam, τὸ ὄν*), Immortal ... At once immense and very subtle, that is this atomic Self" (*bṛhac-ca ... sūkṣmataram ... eṣo'ṇur ātmā,* Muṇḍ. Up. 2. 2. 2 + 3. 1. 7, 9)[32]. This Universal Self, when it inhabits any seed, is "of merely atomic measure" (*aṇu-mātrika,* Manu 1. 56); "that imperceptible minutium (*aṇiman*) that you cannot detect in the seed by dissection, but from which the whole tree grows, that intangible taste as of salt in water, *that* is the Truth (*satyam, τὸ ὄν*), *that* is Self (*ātman*), *that* art thou" (CU. 6. 12, 13): "When a mortal has torn away all that exists (*dharmyam*)[33] and hath obtained Him, the atomic (*aṇum etam āpya*), then is he glad" (KU. 2.13); "less than an atom, greater than immensity" (*aṇor aṇīyān, mahato mahīyān,* KU. 2. 20, Śvet. Up. 3. 20, cf. 5. 9); "less than a grain of rice ... greater than these

[32] On this cf. BrSBh. 2. 3. 19-29 on the *aṇutva* and *mahattva,* minuteness and immensity of the Self. The Yogi who makes himself a master of the elements can reduce himself to this minutium or attain magnitude at will (*Yoga Sūtra* 3. 45).

[33] *Dharmyam* here in its ontological, existential or sensational sense, with reference to "things" (as rightly maintained by Keith, *Religion and Philosophy of the Veda,* 1925, p. 547), and as in the Buddhist propositions, "all things are impermanent" (*sabbe dhammā aniccā,* S. 3. 132 etc.), „things originated causally" (*hetusampannā dhammā,* A. 3. 444).

worlds" (CU. 3. 14. 3); "indivisible, enduring, omnipresent, stable, immoveable, immutable" (*acchedyo*[34] ... *nityaḥ sarvagataḥ sthāṇur acalo* ... *avikāryaḥ*, ʳ ˜ 2.24, 25).

Such formulations are not at all peculiarly Indian: for example, Dionysius explains that "greatness is attributed in the Scriptures to God ... and Smallness, or Rarity" [= *aṇutva* or *sūkṣmatā*] respectively with reference to His transcendance and His immanence (*De div. nom.* 9. 1); and Philo's "the Spirit of God, atomic (τὸ ἄτμητον), indivisible, diffused in its fulness in and through all beings" (*Gig.* 28) is almost verbally identical with the passage cited from the *Bhagavad Gītā.*

If now the ultimate reality,—that Brahma, and Truth, that is the target of our aim (Muṇḍ. Up. 2. 2. 2) —is so minute, if the Janua Coeli[35] is so tiny as to be imperceptible to deluded men and visible only to those who have overcome anger and mastered the powers of the soul (*svargaṁ dvāraṁ susūkṣmam* ... *taṁ tu paśyanti puruṣā jitakrodhā jitendriyāḥ*, Mbh. 14.2784-5, cf. CU. 8. 6. 5, MU. 6. 30), so also must be, and such also is, the Way that leads to and through it, "the ancient narrow (*aṇu* = *sūkṣma*) path whereby the Contemplatives, knowers of Brahma, enter in, liberated hence on high to the world of heavenly-light" (*svargaṁ lokam ita ūrdhvaṁ vimuktāḥ*, BU. 4. 4. 8). The Self, in other words, is the razor-edged Bridge that holds these

[34] *Acchedya*, the literal Skr. equivalent of ἄτομος; although we have also translated *aṇu*, "minute", by "atomic".

[35] For the Janua Coeli see further my "Svayamātṛṇṇā; Janua Coeli" in *Zalmoxis* 2, 1941.

worlds apart and that must be crossed by all who would reach the Farther Shore, trans-etherial, hyperuranian[36]. As in the Christian Gospels: "I am the way ... I am the door ... No man cometh to the Father save by me ... Enter ye in at the strait gate ... Because strait is the gate and narrow is the way which leadeth unto life, and few there be that find it".

It is against the background of all these contexts that we shall have to consider the Buddhist doctrine of the instant moment (*khaṇa* = *ikṣaṇa*, "glance", cf. *nimeṣa*). Before doing so, it should be noted that "time" (*kāla*) is employed in the passages quoted above both in the plural with reference to *periods* of time, and in the singular to denote the *point* of time from which duration extends both backwards and forwards and that is, therefore, at once the beginning and end of time;

---

[36] For the Bridge, see D. L. Coomaraswamy, "The Perilous Bridge of Welfare" in *HJAS*. 8, 1944. Additional references: *Setu vuccati maggo*, VA. 180. RV. 1. 158. 3, V. 84. 2, 7. 35. 13 *(peru)*; TS. 1. 3. 8 *(peru)* and 6. 3. 6. 8 "for he (Agni) is the warden of the waters who is offered up in the sacrifice"; *Bhaktamālā*, "the causeway which God hath built for His liegmen from this world to the next" (Sir G A. Grierson in *JRAS*. 1910, p. 93); BrSBh. 1. 3. 1, 3. 2. 31; in Borneo, *JAOS*. 25; p. 235; M. Smith, *Al-Ghazali the Mystic*, pp. 77, 78, 143 (the Rational Soul "is the Divine bridge stretched between the brutes who are unmixed evil and the angels who are unmixed good. As it descended from the heavens so it will reascend thither and at the last pass away into the Divine Majesty"); H. R. Ellis, *The Road to Hel*, 1943, p. 186 ("golden bridge"); B. de Zoete and W. Spies, *Dance and Drama in Bali*, p. 106; H. B. Alexander, *Mythology of All Races*, X, N. Am. Indian, pp. 6, 273; Nicholson, Rūmī, *Mathnawī* 1. 3700, Commentary (*ṣirāṭ*).

we have distinguished "time" as period from "Time" as principle by the use of the capital for the latter. There is nothing peculiar in the verbal ambiguity of the word *kāla*; it is the same in English and in Arabic, where "time" and *waqt* may refer either to *periods* of time (whether long or short) or precisely to a *point* of time (as when we ask, What time is it *now*?). It may be noted that *kṣaṇa* and *nimeṣa* may refer either to "brief moments" (measurable units of time) or to moments without duration, according to the context[37].

In the latter sense Nimiṣa, "Twinkling of an Eye", as a name of God, is implied by the *naimiṣīyaḥ*, "people of the moment", of CU. 1. 2. 13, where the reference is to sacrificers, and may be compared to the Islamic designation of the true Sufī as *ibnu'l waqt*, "a son of the moment[37a]".

[37] E. W. Hopkins, "Epic Chronology", *JAOS*. 24, 1903, 7-55, cf. *AJP*. 24, 1ff.

[37a] Cf. St. Augustine, *Conf*. 7. 17, where human reasoning finally "in one tremulous stroke of vision arrived at That which Is ... but I could not hold the vision" (pervenit ad id, quod est, in ictu trepidantis aspectus ... sed aciem figere non evalui). This "stroke of vision" corresponds to the "twinkling of an eye" in which the world was created, when God "made all things at once" (*De genesi contra Manicheos* 1. 2. 4 and *De genesi ad litteram* 4. 34. 55),—the "six days" referring only to the logical order of creation, and not to any sequence of divine acts. In other words, God is always creating the world "now, this instant", and it is only to creatures of time that the creation presents itself as a series of events, or "evolution".

For some discussion of these passages see M. H. Carré, *Realists and Nominalists,* Oxford, 1946, p. 7 and John Goheen, *The Problem of Matter and Form in the* De Ente et Essentia *of Thomas Aquinas,* Cambridge, Mass., 1940, pp. 43, 44.

II

BUDDHISM

Early Buddhism, both in the Canon and as interpreted by Buddhaghosa, emphasizes the inconstancy and the extreme brevity of life under any conditions, in a word, its mortality in the sense that "all change is a dying" (Plato, *Euthydemus* 284 D, Eckhart, Evans ed. I. 384); and asserts unequivocally the unreality of "beings" (*satta*)[1] and of the "self" (*attā*)[2], although

[1] S. 1. 135 *evaṁ khandesu santesu hoti satto ti, sammuti . . . nayidha satt' ūpalabbhati;* Mil. 72 *n'atthi koci satto yo imamhā kāyā aññaṁ kāyaṁ saṅkamati;* 268 *na paramatthena satt'ūpaladdhi*. D. 3. 211 *sabbe sattā saṅkhāraṭṭhikā*: S. 1. 97 *sabbe sattā marissanti,*—cf. Aristotle, *De an.* 3. 6 *τὸ γὰρ ψεῦδος ἐν συνθέσει ἀεί*. Just as much as the modern positivist, the Buddhist regards "individuality" as nothing but a transitory association of sensuous data, mere name and phenomenon, and "the very mother of illusions"; *but* at the same time denies absolutely that all that "is my Self". It should be needless to say that the postulated "self" (*attā*) or Ego (*aham*) is other than the Self to which the Buddha "resorts" (S. 3. 143, D. 2. 120), other than the "plenary, great 'I'" (*pūrṇam ahaṁ mahaḥ, Vivekacūḍāmaṇi* 240), other than the "I" that is "proper to none but God in his sameness" (Meister Eckhart). On the two "I's" cf. *JAOS* 67, 1947, pp. 69, 70.

[2] Nothing that can be named or sensed is a real "Self". When the Freedman realises that in the postulated "self" there is no

both are permissible terms when postulated merely for practical, everyday purposes[3].

"Brief is the life of human beings ... none to whom death cometh not" (S. 1. 108, cf. A. 4. 136). Even of a Brahmā, whose day is of a thousand years, is said that "his life is little, not for long" (S. 1. 143). "Life is like a dewdrop... a bubble on the water" (A. 4. 137, cf. D. 2. 246 f.),—"like a dewdrop on the tip of a blade of grass when the sun rises, such is the lifetime of men. Mother! do not hinder me" (Vism. 231), i.e. do not hold me back from the Path. "In the last analysis, the moment of the life (*jīvita-khaṇo*) of beings is just as over-brief (*atiparitto*)[4] as the turning of a single thought; like the turning of a chariot-wheel, which turns by means of just one place on its rim, and stands still by means of only one, so is the life of beings that of a single moment of thought, and when this ends the being is said to have ended. As it has been said, 'In the past thought-moment one lived ... in the future thought-

---

veritable Selfhood, and no longer sees Self in what is not-Self, then he "no longer worries about what is unreal" *(asatā na paritassati,* M. 1. 135).

[3] The pragmatic validity and real invalidity of the postulates corresponds to the distinction of relative, transactional (*vohārika*) and conventional (*sammuti* = *sammata,* or perhaps = *saṁvṛti,* "contingent") from absolute (*paramatthika*) truth. The affirmative language of postulation applies literally only to the world of accidents (D. 2. 63) and can only be employed analogically or negatively to ultimate reality.

[4] Cf. A. 1. 249 where the little self (of which the "life" is referred to above) is *paritto,* the Great Self *aparitto.* On √*ric* see my "*Ūnātiriktau and Atyaricyata*", *NIA.* 6. 52-56.

moment one will live ... in the present thought-moment one is alive',

'Life, the self-ish nature (*atta-bhāva*), pleasure and pain, all [5]
Are conjunct (*samāyutta*) in a single thought, and its moment passes lightly' [6]...

Such is the 'Recollection of Death' in terms of the 'Brevity of the Moment'" (Vism. 238).

"Connatural are life and its theft [7] ... Beings are born bearing in themselves inveteration and death. For indeed their recurrent thinking is infected with inveteration coincidently with its origination; like a stone that falls from a mountain top, it breaks up together with the aggregates of which it is composite, so that instant death (*khaṇika-maraṇam*) [8] is connatural with advent" (Vism. 1. 230). In other words, birth and death are not unique events of any contingent existence, but of the very stuff (*evaṁ-dhammo*) of "life"; and this liability, of which a particular birth and death are only special cases, is precisely that "reincarnation" (*punabbhava, -āgamana*) from which a final escape is sought; im-mortality (*amata*) and life or becoming (*bhava*) are

[5] "All", i.e. the passible five-fold composite "that is not my Self" (*na me so attā*), passim.

[6] *Eka-citta ... vattate* ($\sqrt{vṛt}$) *khaṇo* implying that *citta-vṛtti*, "turning, or inconstancy, of thought" that the Yogi seeks to suppress. The mind is always on the move, and hence often compared to a monkey.

[7] "Theft", i.e. by the "robber", or "waylayer", or "hunter", Death.

[8] Not "sudden death" at the end of one's life, but "instant death" all through it.

not compossibles, but incompatible; "the cessation of becoming is Nibbāna" (S. 2. 117). "As between one thought and the next (*citt'antaro*), such is a mortal" (A. 5. 300): "Could a man be called 'quick' who could so run as to catch in the air arrows loosed at the same time by four master-archers? Quicker than that is the wearing out of the composite-factors of life" (S. 2. 266); "All that is born, whatever is become, is corruptible" (*palokadhammam,* S. 5. 163). It is in this sense that "the Buddha looks upon the world in momentary (*khaṇe khaṇe*) dissolution" (Dpvs. 1. 16)[9].

"Four and eighty thousand aeons the Maruts abide, and yet abide not even for so long as for the sequence of two thoughts... In the present lives the world, and with the break-up of a thought it dies (*paccuppanena jīvati cittabhaṅga mato loke*)[10]... From the unseen come forth born beings, and broken-up pass into the unseen; like a flash of lightning in the ether they arise and pass away" (Vism. 625, 626).

Time (*samaya,* "co-ition") is past (*atīta,* "overgone"), future (*anāgata,* "un-come"), or present (*paccuppanna,* "up-come"). The present has three senses; that of the moment (*khaṇa-*) in which there meet forthcoming, stasis and break-down (*uppāda-ṭṭhiti-bhaṅga-*

[9] Buddhaghosa derives *loka* from *luj, paluj,* to decay, be dissolved (Vism. 427).

[10] Similarly in MU. 6. 17 and 6. 34. 43 "this world, measured by a thought... the conflux, just a thought" (*idaṁ cittamātram... cittam-eva saṁsāram*), i.e. lasts only for so long as a thought, though it may also be meant that it is "of the stuff of thought", conceptual.

pattam); that of the continuation (*santati-*), i.e. "now" in the extended and usual meaning of the word; and that of road (*addhā-*) [11] in the sense of span of life, whether long or short; and of these three presents, the first is included in the second, and the second in the third. The becoming of the five-fold aggregates, i.e. of "beings", or "selves", takes place in the course of all these "times" (Vism. 431, 473).

Observe that the Stasis is only momentary, not in the continuing present, except in the sense that the moments are surrounded by the continuum; "as it might be a mountain torrent flowing swiftly from afar and carrying everything along with it, and there is no moment, pause, or minute (*khaṇo, layo, muhutto*) in which it comes to rest [12],... even so is the life of men

[11] In its most extended sense the Road (*addhā*) as distinct from the Way *(magga)* ... much, indeed, as "byway" from "highway"... is that whole extent of the past habitations (*pubba-nivāsa*) that were "not my Self", but in which, already, more tears have been shed than would fill the sea. "It is through not understanding, failing to penetrate, the Four Ariyan Truths (of Ill, its origin and its eradication, and the Way) that we have run and wandered on this long road,... both you and I... How is a Monk a 'Wayman? In that he is moving fast on this long road to where he has not yet been, there where there is a cessation of all composites, a relinquishing of all conditions, a waning out of thirst, an absence of gust, an arrest of becoming, ... Nibbāna... There is no surcease of Ill until World's End has been reached" (D. 2. 60, A. 3. 164 and 2. 49).

[12] Cf. Plutarch, *Mor.* 432 A, B (on the stream of Time). In my *Figures of Speech or Figures of Thought,* 1946, p. 159, n. 10 (on *kṣaṇika-nairātmādi*) I erred in speaking of existence as "not a continuity but a succession of unique instants

brief and light (*parittaṁ lahukam*)... or like the mark made by a stick on water... For the born there is no 'not dying'"[13] (A. 4. 137). Buddhaghosa's three momentary accidents (*uppāda, ṭhiti, bhaṅga*)[14] are the same as the "forthcoming, maturity, and alteration or dying (*uppāda, vayo, aññathatta*)[15] of things while

of consciousness". The Buddhist doctrine is one of "continuity without identity", and it is because of *both* that the question, Is it the same man or another that reaps what has been sown, cannot be answered by a simple Yes or No.

[13] Aristotle's *τοῦ αὐτοῦ ... καὶ γένεσις καὶ φθορά*, *Met.* 11. 12. 8.

[14] Vism. 404—405; where it is asked whether in the case of one who visits the Brahma-world in an invisible, mental body, he does this "in the moment of the forthcoming or moment of stability or moment of break-up of the resolute thought" of going there, and answered that he goes "in all three moments"; which is as much as to say that they are not three consecutive moments, but one. It has been previously explained that if he goes in a visible body the journey takes some time, "for the body moves slowly".

[15] Aristotle's *αὔξησις*, *ἀκμή*, and *φθίσις*, dependent on food, *De an.* 3. 12; AA. 2. 1. 2 *annena hīmāni sarvāṇi bhūtāni samananti;* Taitt. Up. 2. 2 *annād vai prajā prajāyante;* D. 3. 211 *sabbe sattā āhāraṭṭhikā;* S. 1. 97 *sabbe sattā marissanti.* "All change is a desistance from a nature", Aristotle *Phys.* 4. 13, 222 B, cf. 4. 12, 221 B: "All change is a dying", Plato, *Euthydemus* 283 D, 285 B, and Meister Eckhart (Evans ed. 1. 384); "Alteratio est via ad generationem et corruptionem". St. Thomas Aquinas, *De mixt. elementorum,* ed. Parma 16. 353, cf. *Sum. Theol.* I. 105. 2 and I-II. 113. 7 ad 1.

It can hardly be overlooked, also, that the three phases of existence, *sṛṣṭi, sthiti* and *laya,* that are resumed in every instant, are the respective functions of the Trinity of Brahmā, Vishnu and Śiva in so far as they are logically distinguished from "the unity of the Person".

they last" (*ṭhitānam*) predicated in S. 3. 137, the same, too, as the "procession, stasis and recession" (*gati, sthiti, nivṛtti*) that are synthesised in Time, ŚĀ. 7. 20, and as the "efflux, maturity, and Heimgang" (*srava, vṛddhi, astaṁ gamana*) of which the Time without time, Brahma to wit, is the inexhaustible font (MU. 6. 14); and these three are characteristic of whatever is composite (*saṁkhatam*) but not of what is incomposite (*asaṁkhatam,* A. 1. 152)[16],—and emphatically *not* of the Buddha's "incomposite Eternal-Law" (*asaṁkhataṁ dhammam,* A. 4. 359), *not* of Nibbāna (*asaṁkhatam,* Mil. 270), not of that home (*āyatanam*) "where there is neither coming nor going nor stopping, nor falling nor uprising, no this world and that world, no support, no motion, no inception" nor of that "unborn, unbecome, uncreated, incomposite that *is,* and were it not, there would be no way of escape from the born, become, created and composite" (Ud. 80)[17].

---

[16] Incomposite, i.e. "simple": "intellectus noster... in cognitionem simplicium pervenire non potest, nisi per remotionem compositionis... aeternitas non varietur per praesens, praeteritum et futurum" (St. Thomas Aquinas, *Sum. Theol.* I. 10. 1 and 2, cf. *Sum. contra gentiles* I. 15); "igitur vita eius non habit successionem, sed est *tota simul.* Est igitur sempiterna" (*Sum. contra gentiles* I. 99). I would add, nisi simul, quomodo omnisciens?

[17] It will not be overlooked that all these negative terms, having *nibbāna* and *dhamma* as their reference, are equally such as are applied to God *secundam viam remotionis* in Christianity; cf., for example, *Sum. contra gentiles* I, cc. 14, 15, 18, 23, 89,... God is immutable, incomposite, without accidents, impassible, etc.

Πάντα ῥεῖ: Heracleitus, fr. XLI, "You cannot dip your feet twice into the same rivers; for other waters are ever flowing in": *sabbe dhammā aniccā* (S. 3. 132). That all things—note the plural—are in flux is no more a denial of the real stability of that which is not a "thing" than is the Buddha's destructive analysis of the composite "self", always followed by the words, "that is not my Self", a denial of the Self. As Aristotle (*Met.* 4. 5. 7 and 15f.) points out, there can be "*also* another kind of essence of things that are, wholly devoid of destruction and generation". It cannot be shown that Heracleitus ever explicitly or implicitly denied this; "all things" flow, no doubt, but there is a one and only Wisdom is distinct from "all things" (fr. XVIII),—not one of them; and if, as Ritter and Preller say, the "Ever-living Fire" is such that *unde manat omnis motus,* this does not mean that itself is moved. Aristotle had absolutely no grounds for accusing "these men" of the belief that "sensibilia are the only realities". In Buddhism the reality of an unmoved, incomposite nature is explicitly asserted over against the evanescence of the composite transients; and when Aristotle goes on to say "it is only the realm of sense around us which continues subject to destruction and generation, but this is a practically negligible part of the whole" (*ib.* 22), this might just as well have been said by the Buddha himself!

That there is "no moment in which the river rests" shows clearly that time is not to be thought of as "made of" a succession of stops, but as a continuum (*saṁtāna*); the indivisible moment is immanent in time, but not a part of time; just as for Aristotle "time is not composite of atomic nows, any more than any other magnitude is made up of atoms" (*Phys*. 6. 9. 239 B, cf. 8. 8, 262 A).

Inasmuch as all change is a dying, it is from the inconstancy (*anicca*) of life and thought that the Wayfarer seeks to be emancipated,—"seeking for stability" (*aṭṭhitaṁ nissāya,* A. 3. 219). As we have seen above, Stasis is predicated only in the moment (*khaṇa*) or in the Time (*kāla*) without time that is Brahma—that Brahma and Dhamma that the Freedman, *dhamma-bhūto, brahma-bhūto,* D. 3. 84, S. 3. 93) "has become"; but we have not yet drawn the obvious conclusion that these two are one and the same, though be it noted that in one the past and future *meet,* and from the other *flow,* and that both are *without duration.* What are we, then, to understand by such expressions as "one whose thought is stable" (*ṭhita-citto* D. 2. 157, S. 5. 74) "one whose self is stable" (*ṭhit'attā,* D. 1. 57, S. 3. 55, and notably Sn. 359 *parinibbutaṁ ṭhit'attam*) and "stable, motionless" (*ṭhito anejo,* Th. 1. 372), "as in the ocean's midmost depth no wave is born, but all is still, so for the Monk, who's still and does not move (*ṭhito anejo*), nor should he swell at all"[18] (Sn. 920); or by statements such as that "'having crossed, and reached the Farther Shore (*Nibbāna*), and stands' (*tiṭṭhati*), 'an Arahant' is meant" (S. 4. 175, cf. Sn. 946), or that

---

[18] "Dû solt sîn stête unde veste, daz ist: dû solt gelîch stân liebes und leides, gelükes und ungelükes" (Meister Eckhart, Pfeiffer p. 71).

"having overpast inveteration and death, they 'stand'" (*ṭhassanti*, S. 2. 46)[19].

---

[19] "Stability is the peculiar property of eternity" (Marsilio Ficino, *Commentary on Plato's Symposium* IV. 16). "Men saw these two things [body and soul, i.e. *saviññāna-kāya*], pondered them, investigated both of them, and found that each is mutable in man. The body is mutable in its various ages, in its corruption, its ailments, its reflections and its defections, its life, its death. They passed to the soul, which they certainly comprehended as being the better, and also wondered at as being invisible. But they found it too to be mutable, now willing something, now not willing; now knowing, again not knowing; now remembering, again forgetting; now fearing, again daring; now advancing in wisdom, again relapsing into folly. They saw that it was mutable, they left it too, and went in search of something that should be immutable. And thus they arrived at a cognition of God the Creator by means of the things which He created... Examine the mutations of things and thou wilt everywhere find 'has been' and 'shall be'. Think on God and thou wilt find 'is' where 'has been' and 'will be' cannot be" (St. Augustine, *Sermo* CCXLI. 3. 3 + *In Joan. Evang.* XXXVIII. 10, versions by Erich Przywara, S. J.); further, "clarum est eam [animam] esse mutabilem" (*De ver. rel.* XXX. 54), "non quidem localiter, sed tamen temporaliter" (ib. X. 18); "anima vero jam ipsa crearetur" (*De Gen. ad litt.* VII. 24. 35) and "omnia quae fecit, quia ex nihilo fecit, mutabilia sunt" (*De nat. boni*, I. 1). But "Quod autem incipit aut desinit vivere, vel in vivendo successionem patitur, mutabile est" (St. Thomas Aquinas, *Sum. contra gentiles*, I. 99), and more generally, "whatever has had a beginning must have an end" (Aristotle, *Phys.* 3. 4, 203 B; *Samyutta Nikāya* 4. 46). How, then, can "the" soul be or become "immortal"? Only if, with St. Thomas, Plato, Philo and the Upaniṣads, we recognize that "duo sunt in homine", respectively mortal and immortal by nature,—a created "soul" subject to accidents, and an uncreated "Soul of the soul" above them. St. Augustine asks, in fact, "how

The answer in terms of time is that the Buddha, identified with the Dhamma, must be, like the Dhamma, "simple" (*asaṁkhata,* A. 4. 359) and by the same token "timeless" (*akāliko,* A. 4. 406). The Freedman, in fact, "transcends the aeons"[20] (*kappātīto ... vipamutto,* Sn.

---

is it that reason (*ratio* = λόγος) is immortal, and that I am defined as something both rational and mortal at the same time?" and reflects, "if reason is immortal, and if I who analyze and synthesize all these [temporal] things, am reason, then that by which I am called mortal is not 'mine'... and we ought to fly from the mortal to the immortal" (*De ordine* II. 50).

If we bear in mind that "Dhamma" (*δικαιοσύνη,* Justitia, Lex Aeterna) is one of the Divine Names (*dhamma* and *brahma* being interchangeable terms in the Upaniṣads and the Pali Canon), it will be seen that Augustine's words might as well have been those of the Buddha himself; both were "intensely sensitive to the pathos of mutability". St. Augustine's "then that by which I am called mortal is not mine" corresponds exactly to the Pali *taṁ n'ētam mama, n'eso'ham asmi, na me so attā.*

[20] On the incalculable length of the aeons (*kappa*), in their sequences of hundreds and thousand for which no earliest point can be recognized, see S. 2. 178-193, ending with the words, "Impermanent are all composites the nature of which is to originate and age, and having arisen, then to perish; to have done with them is bliss"

An aeon (*kalpa*) qua *saeculum,* is properly speaking a "day of Brahma" consisting of a thousand yugas or 4320 million human years; in his days and nights successive worlds are manifested and dissolved. The life-span of a Brahmā is a hundred years made up of such days. It is from even this "brief" life that the Buddha teaches a "further escape". But it should be noted that *kappa* (√*kḷp,* related to *kṛ*) is also "concept" or "multiple arrangement", *κόσμος* (cf. RV. 10. 90. 11 *katidhā vi akalpayan?* and conversely MU. 6. 30 *niḥsaṁkalpo*

373), "not a man of the aeons" (*akkapiyo,* Sn. 860); "they call him 'awake' (*buddha*) who discerns the

---

nirabhimānas tiṣṭhet), i.e. *prapañca,* and that just as a Wake is *nippapañca* "unelaborate", so *akappiyo* (Sn. 914 etc.) is not only *ex tempore* but also "other than whatever is conceivable *seriatim*", transcendent not only with respect to "times" but also with respect to temporalia.

The "former habitations" and past aeons are all immediately present to a Buddha who can pounce upon them like a lion or reach them like an arrow its mark; others need to look backward through the ages, one or myriad according to their ability, but a Buddha or Arahant envisages past or future aeons directly (Vism. 411). It as if they formed a circle (beginningless and endless cycle) of which he is the centre, no farther from one than from any other point on the circumference; while others, less adept, must work their way backward along the circumference if they are to see any past time.

When just above (Vism. 410) Buddhaghosa speaks of the remembering of "how *I* was then, So-and-so, of such and such a family, etc.", and of the past conditions as being those "in one's own continuum" (*attano saṁtāne*)—or better, perhaps, "one's own lineage"—this is said "conventionally" (*samuccā*), not in very truth (*paramatthena*); for any well taught Buddhist monk knows better than to ask, What was *I* in a former life, or What am *I* now, or What shall *I* be in the future? For he sees things "as become", i.e. strictly in terms of causal process and only speaks of an "I" for practical convenience in everyday life (S. 2. 26, D. 1. 202). Similarly in D. 1. 81 the analogy of *cuti* and *upapatti* to the case of a man who goes to another village and again returns to his own (the "villages" being this and yonder worlds, as in CU. 8. 6. 2) would be a heresy if taken literally, as is explicit in Pv. 4. 3. 31. The three modalities of personality (*atta-bhāva*), past, present, and future, are mere conventional terms of every speech, not ultimate realities (D. 1. 202). In just the same way for the *Yoga Sūtra* (2. 39 and 4. 35), the contemplation of one's

aeons, the flux of things in which they fall and rise . . ., one for whom birth (*jāti* = *bhava*, *γένεσις*) is at an end" (Sn. 517). For such as these, explicitly, "there is neither past nor future" (*na tassa paccha na purattham atthi*, S. 1. 141); a Buddha's "recollection" does not operate by a following up of the sequences of births and deaths in time, but siezes immediately and

---

former personalities (*ātma-bhāva*) may be a profitable exercise in the earlier stages of a Yogins' development, but one who no longer confuses *sattva* with Self will never propound such questions as "Who was I?", etc. Reincarnation, in other words, is a façon de parler, not really a matter of persistent individualities.

It should be observed that the Buddhist "double truth" (*sammuti-*, *loka-vohāra-*, *loka-niruttiyo*, etc. and on the other hand *paramattha-saccam;* corresponding to the Vedantic *avidyā* and *vidyā*, *vikāra-* and *paramārthika-satyam*), one relative and conventional, the other absolute and certain, correspond to the distinction of metaphysics from "philosophy" (in the narrow sense of the word), and to Plato's distinction of "such knowledge as has a beginning and varies as it is associated with one ore another of the things that wo nowadays call realities" from "the knowledge that abides in that which is absolutely real" (*Phaedrus* 247 E), and distinction of "true opinion" from "truth", parallel to that of becoming from being (*Timaeus* 27 D, 28 A). The *prob*-ability of the relative truths can be established by repeated observation, and such are the statistical "laws of nature" discovered by science; but behind the experience of order "there is a further cause of that which is 'always so'"; it is because of *eternity* that "there never was or will be any *time* when movement was not or will not be"; but such a first cause, being itself uncaused, is not *prob*-able but axiomatic (Aristotle, *Phys.* VIII. 1. 252 B),—i.e. "self-revealing", *sva-prakāśa*, "self-evident".

instantly upon whatever situation in whatever time the Buddha chooses to perceive (Vism. 411); that is to say, all times are present to a Buddha's instant glance.

"Where there is neither past no future" must and can be only *Now*[21]. It is true that for beings in time the momentary now (*khaṇa*) is ever present. But the word, in the sense of "right time" means also op*port*-unity, i.e. *gate*way and although as such this interval[22] is continually opened and closed again as time passes[23], what if the instant opportunity is never seized? From this point of view the Buddha counsels: "Get ye across this sticky-mire, let not the Moment pass (*khaṇo ve mā upaccagā*), for they shall mourn

---

[21] "Ubi futurum et praeteritum coincidunt cum praesenti", Nicolas of Cusa, *De visione Dei*, c. X.

[22] *Inter-vallum:* the "needle's eye" and "strait gate" in the wall of Paradise, "locum ... cinctum contradictoriorum coincidentia, et iste est murus Paradisi, in quo [tu Domine] habitas, cuius portam, custodit spiritus altissimus rationis, qui nisi vincatur, non patebit ingressus" (Nicolas of Cusa, *De visione Dei*, c. IX).

[23] Past and future being, in fact, the Symplegades or Clashing Rocks, and separated only by the now-without-duration through which the Hero (*mahāvīra*) finds his way; in other words, the jambs of the "Doorway of Immortality" (*amatassa dvārā*, M. 1. 226, cf. Vin. 1. 7) that the Buddha (Brahma-become and the Giver of Immortality, A. 4. 226, S. 4. 94) threw open to his followers; and of the Sundoor, of which it is asked, "Who is able (*arhati*, cf. RV. 10. 60. 40 *arhaṇā*) to pass through it",—i.e. is able to take the way of the "unobstructed Sāman, or otherwise, the Lightning" (ib. 1. 30. 2, 4), which "Sāman", as explained above, is to be thought of as the "Harmony" of the past and future forms, *sā* and *ama*.

whose Moment's past"[24] (*khaṇātītā hi socanti,* Sn. 333, cf. Dh. 315, Tha. 403, 653, 1005, Thī. 5, 459); and that he congratulates those of the Monks "whose Moment has been caught" (*khaṇo vo paṭiladdho*) and commiserates those "whose Moment has past" (*khaṇātītā,* S. 4, 126)[25]. Cf. *Anth. Pal.* 16. 275 on the passing Moment.

The moment of release is sudden (*sub-it-aneus,* "going stealthily"): comparable, in fact, to that of an arrow loosed without further effort from the bow to pierce all obstacles and penetrate its mark, being already "that-become" (*tad-bhūta,* i.e. *brahma-bhūta*), when the archer's stance, grip and draw are correct,—the arrow corresponding to the Self and the target to Brahma (Mil. 418 + Muṇḍ. Up. 2. 1. 1—4): and the adequacy of this trope (*upamā*) is so far precise that it extends to the use of the same verbs whether the archer be in fact a bowman or a "target-piercing" (*akkhaṇa-vedhin*)[26] Monk,—viz. *saṁdhā,* "synthesise" applied to the setting up of the bow and the placing (*yoga*) of the arrow, which can

---

[24] Almost exactly as William Blake's:

> "... he who kisses the joy as it flies
> Lives in eternity's sunrise...
> But, if once you let the ripe moment go,
> You can never wipe off the tears of woe".

[25] It must not be overlooked, of course, that *khaṇa* has also the meaning of "opportunity" present during a relatively short *period* of time; as in Thī. 459 where Sumedhā says, "This is an age of the Buddhas; gone is the absence of opportunity, the moment's siezed!" (*virajjito akkhaṇo, khaṇo laddho*).

[26] *Akkhaṇa* = Skr. *ākhaṇa,* "target", in JUB. 1. 60. 7, 8 and CU. I. 2. 7, 8; and is not to be connected etymologically with *khaṇa,* "moment".

therefore be thought of as "in *samādhi*" [2], *muc*, "loose", with reference to the liberation of the arrow or the Self, and *vyadh*, "penetrate" (in some forms identical with *vid*, "know" or "find") with reference to the attainment of the archer's "aim" [27].

In the case of the Buddha and some other Arahants (cf. Tha. 173, Thī. 627) the Awakening takes place at dawn, that is to say at a junction of times (*saṁdhi*), or twilight, when it is neither night (the prior form) nor day (the posterior form); and in this connection it is not insignificant that a synonym for *saṁdhi* is *brahma-bhūti*, "becoming Brahma". Even at any point of time, the event takes place at a conjunction of times past and future, and it is not without interest that the word *yoga* in its astronomical sense can be substituted for the "moment" of Awakening (Thī. 4). The suddenness of the Awakening contrasts with the length of the Way, the aeonic time that is *now* and once for all escaped (much as the sudden release of the arrow contrasts with the archer's long training); and this is especially emphasized in the Mahāyāna, notably in Vasubandhu's *Abhisamayālaṇkāra*, where when the end of the long road has been reached, the Great Awakening (*abhi-saṁbodhi*) is "single-instantaneous" (*eka-kṣaṇa-*) [28].

[27] See further my "Symbolism of Archery" in *Ars Islamica* 10, 1943.

[28] E. Obermiller, "The Doctrine of Prajñā-pāramitā as exposed in the Abhisamayālaṁkāra of Maitreya", *Acta Orientalia* 11, 1933, pp. 81, 82. Abhi-samaya, "full attainment", may be more literally something like "super-coincidence", as of "time" considered absolutely; cf. also *samayaitum* (co-ire). to "pass through" (the midst of the Sun), JUB. I. 6. 1, suggesting an

The notion of "instantanous [i.e. timeless] awakening" (*ekakṣaṇābhisambodhi*) persists also in Tantrik Buddhism, where it is given, quite logically, a double signifance, comparable to that of a point on the circumference of a circle, such a point being at one and the same time its beginning and end, alpha and omega. As beginning, the awakening is the instantaneous quickening[29] from which the development of the embryo proceeds to the conscious perception of the "net of contingency" (*māyājāla*) in the dimensioned (*nirmāṇa-*) body. On the other hand, as already explained above, the instant or timeless Wakefulness from which generation (the descent of spirit into matter) proceeds is not only the first but also the last moment of the temporal cycle (*kāla-cakra*) of existence (*saṁsāra*), when consciousness returns to its source; evolution (*utpatti-krama* = *pravṛtti*) and involution (*utpannakrama* =

---

equation of *abhisamaya* with *parāyaṇa.* I substitute "single-instantaneous" for Obermiller's "momentary" because the latter word could be understood to mean "ephemeral" or "transient", which is not intended; "momentary" would be right for *khaṇe khaṇe,* but not for *eka-kṣaṇe. Eka-kṣaṇa-* corresponds to Śaṅkara's *sadya* in *sadyo-mukti,* BrSBh. 1. 1. 11; *sadya,* "this day", like *sakṛt,* "forthwith", "no sooner than", etc., cf. St. Augustine, *De lib. arb.* III. 25. 77 Millia dierum in temporis mutibilitate intelligantur; unus autem diei nomine incommutibilitas aeternitatis vocatur.

[29] Cf. Manu I. 56 "When [the Great Self] becoming atomic (*aṇumātriko bhūtvā*) and with a view to existence and motion inhabits the seed with which it is associated, then it assumes an actual-form (*mūrtiṁ vimuñcati*)". The Tantra asserts the intemporal, Manu the undimensioned quality of the animating principle.

nivṛtti) representing the two halves of the cycle of existence, whether cosmic or individual. So in yoga practise, of which the purpose is involutionary, we find a contemplation on time, directed towards the immediate realisation of ever greater and greater durations and pursued until the whole of time can be experienced *now*. Inspiration and expiration [30] are correlated successively with day and night, fortnights, months, and so on, the procedure culminating in "a complete resolution of microcosmic time by the disciple who, having successively fixed his mind on ever greater periods of time and successively rid himself of them in the course of his breathing, comes at length to the great universal aevum; including all creation from its beginning to its reabsorption",—or rather, regeneration (palingenesis), for "this is the yogic rebirth, briefly and clearly described in the following quotation from *Kālacakratantra*: 'The birthplace of the Royal Conquerors is in one constant moment (*ekasmin-samaye'kṣare*) [31]; when the 'heart' is established in the

[30] In Yoga practise, the in- and out-breaths are equated or identified, each being sacrificed in the other (BG. 4. 29, 5.27); and that is, in the last analysis a realisation of the Supreme Identity of Mitrāvaruṇau, who are both the in-and-out-breaths (ŚB. 1. 8. 3. 12) and day and night (TS. 2. 1. 74), and of the Unity of the Gale (Vāyu) "who blows as one, but in man becomes these two, the in-and out-breathing" (ŚB. 1. 8. 3. 12), "who bestows these breaths" (TS. 2. 1. 1. 3) and is in fact the "other whereby men live" (KU. 5. 5).

[31] *Akṣara*, "still", "not fluent", from a Hindu point of view, a designation of Brahma, and of the syllable OM by which he is represented in verbal iconography.

Great Breath, and actual breathing has ceased, when the physical sense-powers are relinquished and the divine have arisen, when the natural planes have been left and the planes divine are seen, then I see All, Great King, then there is naught that is not always seen'". Having thus realised his own-nature or intrinsic being (*svabhāva*), become what he is, the Yogī "without any subjective-objective relation ... knows all because it [his essence] comprehends all in a geometric point (*bindu*) and in one instant (*eka-kṣaṇa*) ... Time is drowned in eternity" [32].

Such a "control of the moments and their sequence" (*Yoga Sūtra* 3.52) as this is the contemplative equivalent of the Vedic seasonal sacrifices by which Prajāpati, the Year (Time) having been, by the act of creation, unstrung and dismembered into the parts of the year (time), i.e. days and nights, etc., of which the conjunctions are his broken "joints", is made whole and complete again [33], at the same time that the Sacrificer himself is reintegrated (*Śatapatha Br.* 1.6.3.35 and passim). "For because the year is a counterpart

---

[32] Mario E. Carelli, *Sekoddeśaṭīkā,* Baroda, 1941, Introduction pp. 16, 17 and Skr. text p. 7 (but the version of the *Kālacakratantra* passage is my own).

[33] These "joints" (*parvāṇi*) are (in a surgical sense) "reset", or literally "put together" or "syn-thesised", cf. AĀ. 7. 20, where Time unites (*saṁdadhāti*) past, present and future times. Things thus put together (*saṁhita*) are in *samādhi,* in wholeness or health; and this completes the cycle that began with their division and sickness (*vyādhi*). The separative act of creation is necessarily followed by the unitive (re-collective) process of involution; complication by simplification.

(image) of Prajāpati, they call him the Year" (*ibid.* 11. 1. 6. 13); "the Year is everything, and that is what 'Imperishable' means" (*ibid.* 11. 1. 2. 12). "How many days are there in the year?" That depends upon the way it is divided, but "really, only one; the Year is just that day after day"; and the Comprehensor of this doctrine of the Year himself becomes the Year" (*ibid.* 12. 2. 2. 23).

Except for the last references, the doctrine of the "Now that stands" has been dealt with so far only on the basis of the Hinayāna. Many other scholars, notably Jacobi, Keith [34], De la Vallée Poussin, and Stcherbatsky, have studied it only from the Mahāyāna sources, in which it is expanded, but certainly did not originate. All schools, of course, retain the doctrine of the causal efficacy of the past operative in the present. Keith, indeed, always assuming that the Buddha denied the reality of the Self—which he never did, but rather counselled men to "seek for" and "take refuge" in it (Vin. 1. 23, Vism. 393, D. II. 120, S. 3. 143)—goes so far as to say that the Vaibhāsika doctrine "interpolates the moment of existence (*sthiti*), which, it asserts, was suppressed by the Buddha be-

[34] Although Keith himself asks respecting the Buddha's "unfathomable" nature predicated in S. 4. 374, etc., whether this "is not to argue that the Tathāgata apart from the mortal constituents is something real but ineffable?" and calls it "unwise to insist on seeing negativism in passages where another explanation is not merely possible, but probably more in accordance with the ideas of the teachers of the early Canon" (*Buddhist Philosophy in India and Ceylon*, 1923, p. 26).

cause of the danger which it involved to the doctrine of impermanence"[35]; implausible, because the notion of a "permanent" Self and "impermanent" self involves no antinomy, and in any case the word *ṭhiti*, even in combination with *attā*, is by no means avoided in the Canon, where also the verbs *ṭitthanti* and *ṭhassanti* (as cited above) are used of Arahants; nor can there be any question but that the Dhamma, with which the Buddha identified himself is an "eternal substance" (*akāliko dhātu*). For the Sautrāntikas, whose very name implies their orthodoxy, "the true doctrine is that there is no distinction between the entity, the efficiency, and the time of its appearance; entities appear from non-existence[36]; they exist for a moment; then they cease to exist. Their existence, activity, and action are

---

[35] A. B. Keith, *ibid.* p. 167.

[36] "Which temporal things before they are, are not; and when they are, pass away; and when they are passed away, will not be. And so, when they are future, they are not yet; and when past, no longer are" (St. Augustine, *De lib. arb.* 3. 7. 21).

In RV. 10. 72, 2 *asataḥ sad ajāyata,* "the existent springs from non-existence", cf. CU. 3. 19. 1, Taitt. Up. 2. 7, where "non-existent" means "not yet existing", "being in potentiality", *prāgabhāva.* On the other hand, in the contrary formulae of TS. 4. 6. 1. 2, CU. 6. 2. 1, 2 and BrSBh. 2. 1. 17, 18, where being arises only from being, "not from the non-existent", the reference is to the fourth, *atyanta,* absolute, kind of non-existence, that of things that could never be, e.g. "the son of a barren woman". In Aristotelian terms, "appearance from non-existence (*prāgabhāva*)" would be "reduction from potentiality to act", and this is the sense in the beautiful prayer of BU. 1. 3. 28, *asato mā sad gamaya,* "Lead me from non-existence unto existence". Cf. also *JAOS.* 66. 154, n. 30.

all one... Past and future are mere names"[37]. All this involves, of course, the old doctrine of the Void (*śūnyatā*)[38] which Keith discusses in connection with the

---

[37] A. B. Keith, *ibid.* p. 166. Rūmī, *Mathnawī* 1. 2201, "Past and future are to thee a curtain from God".

[38] Just as in the case of "destruction" (*khaya*) it must be asked, if the "Annihilationist Heresy" (*ucchedavāda*) is to be avoided, just what can and should be destroyed (Vism. 508), and as in the case of "escape" (*nissaraṇam*) it must be asked, From what, and To what, if we are to know what is meant, so in the case of the "void" (*suññam*) it must be asked, Of what? As Hermes Trismegistos says, "you must not call anything 'void', without saying what the thing in question is void of" (Ascl. III. 33 C); cf. Aristotle, who points out that "to determine whether the 'void' (τὸ κενόν) 'is' or 'is not' we must know what those who use the word really mean by it. The current answer is, 'a place in which there is nothing'. But that is the explanation given by those who hold that nothing 'is' but 'matter' (σῶμα), that which is 'tangible' (ἁπτόν)... and yet no one supposes that they are thinking of the 'point' (ἡ στιγμή), to which the definition really applies" (*Phys.* 4. 7, 213 B-213 A). It is only because such questions are not asked that so many a modern recoils from what he calls the "negativity" of Buddhist formulae; in reality, this *via negativa* implies a "transvaluation" of values, and not their destruction, and what the modern empiricist and "optimist" really resents is precisely the sacrifice that any transvaluation of values demands.

The Buddhist "Void" is empty of things that become and to which the language of affirmative empiricism really applies (D. 2. 63). "Freedom", though a good, is always a freedom *from* limitations, or "de-*void*" of them.

On various senses of the term *suññatā* see Vism. 512. Note also that "Void" and "Plenum" are never unrelated, but rather coincide, cf. Aristotle *Met.* 1. 4. 9, 4. 5. 5, and references in my

Mādhyamikas, or Middle-Waymen, whose name again asserts their orthodoxy. For them "the doctrine of causation must he taken as referring only to the world of ignorance", i.e. opinion. This I take not only to mean that things only *happen* in time and space but also that cause and effect are not only transcendentally but actually always simultaneous; we think of cause and effect as precedent and sequent because all logical formulation applies, in so far as language (the language of postulation) is employed affirmatively only to events (D. 1. 202). So we find it uneasy to understand just how a cause can operate at a distance [39]; how, if things exist only for a moment, can they work on one another? How can their order be explained? In fact, if we presume that acts are causes, then the orderly sequence of events will have to be explained by a "pre-established harmony", arbitrarily established; and this was the false position, into which the Islamic Mutakallemin

---

"Kha and other words denoting Zero ...", *BSOS*. 7, 1934, pp. 487—497. This coincidence is implied by the Mahāyāna aphorism, *yas saṁsāras tan nirvāṇam,* and the words of the *Īśvara Pratyabhijñā Vimarśinī,* 1. 193, *yac cid viśeṣatvaṁ tad sadāśivatattvam* are only saying the same in other words.

[39] For example, when a plant, transferred from its original environment to another and different set of conditions, continues to flower in "its own" time regardless of the new conditions, this represents in it the working of a kind of memory that, as such, is "imperceptible" (*adṛṣṭa*) to human beings, who can investigate the distant causes in the plants original environment, but cannot "see" them as they still actually exist in the plant, in which cause and effet coincide at every "moment" of its growth.

were forced by the logic of their own kind of atomism. The answer to all these difficulties is that causes never operate at a distance, but *are present* when and where their effects are seen [40]. Nothing of an act outlasts the act itself; but the actions leaves its trace in the environment, which will for ever afterwards be other than it would have been if the event had not taken place; the act and its causal efficacy are two different things, of which one (which is perceptible) and the other (which can only be inferred) persists. It stands to the high credit of Indian logic to have distinguished acts (*karma*) from causes (*kāraṇa*), and to have given the significant names of "unseen" (*adṛṣṭa*) and "not-past" (*apūrva*) to "causality"; the latter term, in particular, at the same time implying that the efficacy of an act (unlike the act itself) is really *present-when* the effect appears; the consequences of past actions always remaining latent until the conditions under which they can operate arise. From this point of view there remains no inconsistency in a combination of the concept of instant actuality with the operation of mediate causes in time.

On the other hand, it would be obviously impossible to apply the causal formula, that the efficacy of the

---

[40] So it is that, as St. Thomas Aquinas says, "fate lies in the created causes themselves" (*Sum. Theol.* 1. 116. 2). The deduction will naturally follow that, to escape from fate, to be free, which is to fulfil one's destiny (reach one's destination, man's last end), one must have "denied himself" (*denegat seipsum*, Math. 16. 24) and passed over from becoming to being.

cause is really *present-when* the effect appears, the consequences of past actions always remaining latent until the conditions under which they can operate are established; whereas, the causal act and its effects are never simultaneous, however soon the latter may be realised.

On the other hand, it would be obviously impossible to apply the causal formula, "this being so, that follows", to that other world in which there is no becoming and no triad of origination, existence, and decay to be accounted for. Keith continues: "Absolute reality, Çāntideva points out, does not fall within the domain of the intellect (*buddhi*), for that moves in the realm of relativity and error. Nāgārjuna denies consistently that he has any thesis of his own, for to uphold one would be wholly erroneous; the truth is silence, which is neither affirmation nor negation"[41]. All of these are positions already established in the Hīnayāna Canon[42].

---

[41] A. B. Keith, *ibid.* pp. 235-239.

[42] Just as for Śaṅkara "this Brahma is silence" (BrSBh. 3. 2. 17): "Whom only silence can declare" (Hermes Trismegistos, I. 31, cf. X. 5): "Nothing true can be said of God" (Meister Eckhart in Evans, 1. 87, citing St. Augustine, cf. Kena Up. I and II). Silence is the "Middle Way" between affirmation and negation; and corresponds to that "untold" (*anakkhātam,* Dh. 218, *avyākatam,* S. 4. 374f.) which the Buddha, for all that he "holds nothing back", cannot reveal for lack of any "speechway" (*vādapatha*). Silence is a "Middle Way" between affirmation and negation; and what is probably the oldest text on Silence in this sense is to be found in the verses quoted in AĀ. 2. 3. 8, v. 3:

De la Vallée Poussin[43] discusses *kṣaṇa* (1) as a measure of time and (2) as the limiting minimum of

---

"Of speech, that which is 'yes' and which is 'no'...
Discarding, the prophets (*kavayaḥ*) found -their-quest;
[Erst] bound by names, [now] they delighted in audition (*śruti*).

The Buddha characteristically "discards the yes and no" when he so often says that the condition of a Freedman, Arahant, post mortem, cannot be described by such expressions as "is" or "is not" or by any copulative or disjunctive combination of these expressions,—just as, for the Upanispads, the Self is *neti, neti.* The Buddha, moreover, likewise denies that he has any "views" (Sn. 837, cf. 152 and 878f., 914).

One further reservation must be made: the Buddhist doctrine of Causality (*hetuvāda,* literally "etio-logy") refers only to the operation of natural or mediate causes, or in other words to necessity; the same applies to the Western doctrine of causality as formulated by Leukippos (Aetios, I. 25. 4): for Plato, *Timaeus* 28 a, "everything becomes from some cause, of necessity"; and so on, to the scholastic doctrine that "nothing happens by chance" (St. Augustine *QQ LXXXIII,* q. 24) and the modern scientist's "faith" in order. Past events determine the character of any entity at any given moment, and in this sense "fate lies in the created causes themselves" (St. Thomas Aquinas, *Sum. Theol.* I. 116. 2). But this no more in Buddhism (or Islam) than in Christianity excludes the entity's responsibility for what, out of the bundle of possibilities that it inherits, it *elects* to do. Otherwise, all the Buddha's exhortations to do this (*kiriyavāda*) and not to do that (*akiriyavāda*), to eradicate this and to make that become, and the whole concept of "self-control" (the conquest, control or management, and impulsion of self by Self, Dh. 104, 160, 379 *attanā codāy'attānam,* 390 and passim) would be meaningless. It is true that all the reactions of the self or Ego are fated and determined by past causes, but all that "is not my Self" (*na me so attā,* passim), and whoever does not identify himself with it is in a position time, analogous to the atom (*paramāṇu*) considered as an indivisible minimum of "matter"; he barely mentions Hīnayāna sources, and ignores their background altogether, though he quotes Vasubandhu on S. 2. 265. He cites various definitions of the moment in which a thing (*dhamma*)[44] exists, all amounting to this, that the moment has no real duration; it is just as incalculably short as the sum of the aeons would be incalculably long; a moment is simply the indivisible present in which the three phases of any existence take place,—"on ne peut douter que... le *kṣaṇa,* durée du Dharma [chose] soit une grandeur de temps se rapprochant de zéro à l'infinité". At the same time it does not seem to me correct to say that "le temps est discontinu et fait de *kṣaṇas,* comme le corps étendu est fait d'atomes", because the interval between two *kṣaṇas* is no more than the *kṣaṇa* itself a period, and in the same way the space between two atoms is no larger than the measure of an atom, which is nil[45]. Time flows

---

to make *it* behave as *ne* will. This is not an interference with the operation of causality; it is simply that with "repentance", i.e. "change of mind", previously inoperative causes are brought into play, with new results.

[43] "Notes sur le 'moment' ou *kṣaṇa* des bouddhistes", *Rocznik Orientalisticzny,* 8, 1931, 1-13, in which he quotes from his own version of Vasubandhu's *Abhidharmakośa* and from other sources.

[44] Dhamma as "thing", a very common meaning also in the Pali sources, must not be confused with Dhamma as "Eternal Law" and (in *sa-dhamma*) "Natural Law".

[45] Aristotle deals with the problem in much the same way (Phys. IV. 13. 222 a, b): time is "always beginning" (ἀεὶ γὰρ ἐν

in the same way that a river flows, continuously, and never rests (*na ramati*). Poussin cites also some Jaina sources[46] in which *samaya* as point of time corresponds to the Buddhist *kṣaṇa*: "a moment (*samaya*) is the minimum time (*kāla*) required by an atom (*paramāṇu*) to move its own length", and "a moment is the time required by an atom to pass through the interval between two atoms" (*aṇvantaram*)[47].

Stcherbatsky's treatment of the Moment, in *Buddhist Logic*[48] is fuller, and he does recognize that "the origin of the theory of Instantaneous Being is probably pre-Buddhistic"[49]. He observes that for the Buddhist "existence and non-existence are not different appearances *of* a thing, they are the thing itself", quoting

---

ἀρχή): it is by means of the indivisible now (ἄτομος νῦν) that "time is continuous"; in one sense the nows are different from one another, but in their function of holding time together they are "always the same" (ἀεὶ τὸ αὐτό).

"Moments" are like "points" determining a line; two contiguous points will not make a line, but only three, because a line is not a line unless it has a beginning, middle and end; and so with all other series.

[46] *Tattvārthādhigama*, treated by H. Jacobi in ZDMG. 40; and *Gaṇitasārasaṁgraha*, edited by M. Rangacharya, Madras, 1912

[47] *Aṇvantara*, cf. *citt'antara* cited above, and *buddh'antara*, "interval between two successive advents", is neither Rangacharya's "un autre atome" nor Poussin's "l'intervalle, l'étendu d'une atome".

[48] *Bibliographica Buddhica* XXVI, 2 vols, Leningrad, 1930, 1932.

[49] Stcherbatsky does not go very far back. In a footnote he says: "The Sānkhya-Yoga in this point, as in many others, comes very near to the Buddhist view, cp. Vyāsa on III. 52—*kālo vastu-śūnya-buddhi-nirmāṇaḥ sarva-jñāna-anupātī, kṣaṇas-*

Śantarakṣita, "the nature of anything is its own momentary stasis and destruction" (*yo hi bhāvaḥ kṣaṇa-sthāyi vināśa iti giyate, Tattvasangraha* p. 137.26). Such a destruction is not, of course, the empirical event that takes place when the jar is shattered by a blow and is then no longer a jar, but as much intrinsic to the thing as is is very existence (pp. 94, 95).

Stcherbatsky is right in saying that, in Vasubandhu's words, "because of immediate destruction, there is no (real) motion" (*na gatir nāśāt, Abhidhammakośa* 4.1)[50] and would have been right in emphasizing that motion itself, and therewith time, is only a pragmatic postulate—just as for Buddhists the Ego, individuality, is only a pragmatic postulate—and as a concept, not an external reality but something constructed by ourselves, whose manner of knowing is in terms of time and space,—Kant's "forms of our intellect". But he is not right in deducing from this that "motion is discontinuous"; for, on the one hand, motion is, experientially, continuous, and as we have seen, "the river never stops"; while on the other, there is no motion really; and neither of these propositions, respectively relative and absolute, involves a discontinuity such as would be involved if we relapsed into the fallacy of thinking of a line as "made up of" points. Vasubandhu illustrates his position (as Rūmī did) by the example of a moving light, which produces the appearance of a line

---

tu vastu patitaḥ", which I take to mean that time is a baseless mental construction, and a derivative of the moment.

50 See in L. de la Vallée Poussin, *L'Abhidharmakośa de Vasubandhu*, 5. vols., Paris 1923-1931.

of light, and "moves" in the same sense that we speak of a man as "walking". But Tscherbatsky[51] is wrong in saying (p. 99) that the so-called "motion consists of a series of immobilities". What Vasubandhu actually says is that "the arising of instants is untinter-

---

[51] Tscherbatsky goes on to discuss "some European parallels", chiefly in Bergson. He cites "the world that the mathematician deals with is a world that dies and is reborn every instant, the world which Descartes was thinking of when he spoke of continuous creation" (*Creative Evolution*, pp. 23, 24) and "the Ego has no reality... It is an endless flow" (*ib.* pp. 3, 4), and "the proposition that movement is made out of immobilities is absurd" (ib. p. 326). But when he (Tscherbatsky) sums up (p. 118) by saying "for the Buddhists there are no stops at all other than in imagination, the universal motion never stops... for Bergson, on the contrary, real is duration, the moments are artificial cuts in it", I am unable to understand in what respect there is a contradiction.

For Leibniz there may be consulted F. S. C. Northrop, "Leibniz's Theory of Space" in *JHI*. 7, 1946. Leibniz denies "the void in space, atoms, and even particles not actually divided. And, further, he distinguished two levels of truth, that of "the primary truths of fact" (amongst which are propositions relating to the self) and "the truths of reason" (axiomatic propositions, e.g. that "every spirit... is durable and absolute"),—all of which "has the consequence of making matter as known by any scientific knower or observer purely phenomenal". There is a certain irony, on the other hand, in the fact that for a typical modern nominalist such as A. B. Keith, "such knowledge as is not empirical is meaningless, and ought not to be described as knowledge" (*Aitareya Āraṇyaka,* 1909, p. 42); this last position has been destructively analysed by Wilbur M. Urban, who concludes that "the metaphysical idiom of the Great Tradition is the only language that *is* really intelligible" (*The Intelligible World,* 1929, p. 471)!

rupted" (*nirantara-kṣaṇa-utpāda*); and the word that Tscherbatsky renders by "series" is actually *saṁtāna*[52], which is literally and etymologically a "continuum", and what he says is that "'lamp' is the name conventionally given to a continuum of lights so as to make a sort of unity", and that it is just in the same way that "this man, So-and-so's" name is conventionally given to what is really a continuing process, not a substantial "self". And herein there is no departure from early Buddhist doctrine in which *punar utpadāna* is already explained in terms of the lighting of one lamp from another, and there is no essence (*sattā*) that moves on. In any case, any division of the continuity of time into a series of immobile instants would be just as artifical as a division of time into a discontinuous series of hours or days, or as the division of a line into a series of points; one might as well think of time as a thing *created* by the jerky motion of the hands of a clock!

[52] It is precisely this continuity (*saṁtāna,* which Dasgupta also misrenders by "series") that enables Cakrapāṇi to say that although the existence of the body is momentary (*kṣaṇika*), the connection of the Supreme Self with the body is not intermittent but constant (Comment on *Caraka-saṁhitā* 1. 1. 41). It is significant here, also, that Cakrapāṇi so well observes that "the constancy (or eternity) of the Self is a matter of its concurrence with its own past and future hypostatic experiences" (*nityatvaṁ cātmanaḥ pūrvāparāvasthānubhūtārtha-pratisaṁdhanāt,* Comment on 1. 1. 55), i.e. inasmuch as It is the one and only transmigrant. Thus what is for one a proof of the pseudo-identity of the transient self is for the other a proof of the real identity of the constant Self; and these are complementary, and by no means contradictory, propositions.

III

GREECE

In discussing Time and Eternity in Greek contexts I shall refrain from entering into any long account of Greek "atomism" as a whole; since it appears that a distinction must be made between the physical atoms of which bodies may be a composite, and the atomic time that divides and unites periods of time from and to one another, just as the point divides or unites parts of a line from or to one another. Physical atoms must have some dimension, however small, if anything is to be "made of" them; but the time-atom is a zero, and explicitly "not a part of time". It would be truer (though not exact) to say that past and future are parts of the time-atom than it would be to describe a period of time as "made up of" time-atoms; just as the point is the principle and sine qua non of extension, but points, having no extension, cannot be added up to make a length, and we cannot say that extended things are "made up of" points. And so, with perfect logic, Plato does not speak of the elements as "atomic", but only as existing in particles "so very small as to be invisible", and only forming visible masses when these particles are assembled in sufficient numbers (*Timaeus* 56 C).

Aristotle, similarly, though an "atomic now" and "indivisible point" are essential to his thinking (*Phys.* 6. 3. 234 A), is not an "atomist" in the material sense; he knows that "nothing continuous can be made of atoms" (ἐξ ἀτόμων), and that "all magnitude is continuous" (*Phys.* 232 A, cf. 241 B): atoms have *no* magnitude, and one cannot speak of atoms "next to" one another because what lies between two points is always a dimension (if not, they would be one and the same point), *Phys.* 231 A, B + 8. 8, 264 A, cf. 241 A. Our concern is only with the really and absolutely indivisible and undimensioned atom or point that gives a meaning to time or space [1], and not at all with such "atoms" as have now been actually "split", or with those of the "atomists" such as Leukippos for whom "there are an infinite number of them, and they are invisible owing to the smallness of their bulk" (Aristotle, *De gen. corr.* A, 8. 324 b 35) [2]; atoms that are "not mathematically indivisible", but each of which "*has magnitude*" and extension [3], and of which, therefore, perceptible things *can* be constituted,—atoms that can, in fact, only be so called for so long as men have not yet been able to divide them, and which are really only *particles* [4].

[1] "Non-spatial and non-temporal intuition is the condition of the interpretation of the space-time world itself" (W. M. Urban, *The Intelligible World,* p. 260).

[2] As cited by Burnet, *Early Greek Philosophy,* 4th ed. p. 335.

[3] J. Burnet, l. c. p. 336.

[4] And can therefore, quite logically, be thought of as constituent parts of great magnitudes. Atomic constitution implies, indeed, a discontinuity of matter, but does not require a dis-

Before Aristotle, Parmenides (Diels fr. 8 preserved by Simplicius) had set forth in the clearest possible terms the doctrine that "that which *is*", and being Now, is other than the things that only seem to be and since they come into being and pass away, cannot be said to *be*. This indivisible, omnipresent and altogether present One is unoriginated and indestructible; "it is complete, immoveable, and endless. Nor *was* it ever, nor *will* it be for Now it *is*, all at once, a continuous One... It is all alike... without beginning or end, since coming into being and passing away are excluded and far away from it, and true belief rejects them". When he goes on to say that "it cannot be called 'infinite', because it is in need of nothing", this sounds strange to us, but only means that it is not a void or chaos but a plenum, only "finite" in the sense that it is self-contained. And if he also calls the One a "sphere, equally poised from the centre in every direction; for it cannot be greater or smaller in one place than another", this implication of a bounding circumference (as it were dividing the light from the outer darkness), is no more inconsistent with the concept of an immaterial essence than is St. Bonaventura's thought of God as a circle of which the centre is everywhere and the circumference nowhere (*Itin. mentis* 5).

---

continuity of the space in which they must be thought of as arranged, nor does it require that this space should be literally a void. All traditions speak of an original separation of heaven and earth, in order that there may be a room or space in which things can exist; but the space thus created is aerial rather than empty.

Parmenides goes on to say that that which *is* is what is true; and to contrast it with the world of mortal opinion that is characterised by opposite forms, the contraries, of which light and darkness are the types, of which he also says that one should be ignored, since it is merely a privation of the other, and being therefore an un-reality cannot be thought. Aristotle, to be sure, in *De caelo* 1. 298 b 21, asserts that Parmenides is speaking all the time only about a sensible reality; but how could that be true of a description that expressly excludes an existence in time, and the realm of the contraries, which is itself the world of "sensible reality"? Indubitably, Parmenides is speaking of the Essence that others call "God", and it is significant that he not only enunciates the Now-ness of the One that is, but can only define it by negations of all that it is not.

For Plato, the world was made by Zeus according to a self-same, stable, living paradigm, not generated but eternal (*ἀΐδιος*); and as it would have been impossible to attach the quality of Eternity wholly to what was generated[5], "he designed to make out of Eternity (*αἰών*, Skr. *āyus*, 'life') a something moving; and so, when He was ordering the whole Heaven (Universe), He made out of that Eternity that ever abides in its own unity a sempiternal (*αἰώνιος*) image, moving

[5] An image is never like its archetype in all respects, or would be not an image, but a duplicate (*Cratylus* 432 C, D); in the present case the point is that "generation" and "eternity" are incompatibles.

according to number [6], even that which we have called 'time' (χρόνος)[7]. For simultaneously He contrived the days and nights, and months and years, that were not before the generation of the Heaven (Universe) [8]. And

[6] Cf. Skr. *jagat,* "the moving" i.e. the world. It should be noted, however, that motion includes "rest", which is not the same thing as "immoveability", but only a potential and temporarily inhibited motion; not to mention that things "at rest" are not thereby exempted from change and alteration. As Aristotle says, "Nature is the principle (or origin) of rest as well as motion", both of which are "in time" (*Phys.* 8. 3, 253 B + 6. 8, 239 A, 4. 12, 221 B) and impossible in the "now" (*ib.* 6. 3. 234 A): and our present concern is with this timeless "Nature" (Plato's διαιώνια φύσις, *Timaeus* 37 B) as distinguished from its temporal manifestations, which is the distinction of the stasis of that which *is* from the motion-and-rest of things that *become.* This distinction is made already in RV. 1. 115. 1 where the Sun is the Self (principle) of "all that is in motion or at rest" (*jagatas tasthuṣaś-ca*). Following Aristotle, St. Thomas (*Sum. Theol.* 1. 10. 4 ad 3) also points out that time "not only measures motion, but also rest".

[7] Κρόνος, the father of Zeus, was later on assimilated to χρόνος, "time", although this is etymologically inconceivable. It is, in fact, Zeus, who, like Prajāpati, can be equated with the Year, and must be identified with time; that he overthrew his father means that, *qua* time, he subdivided Time; while that Kronos swallowed all his children, Zeus excepted, only means that Eternity is both the source of all times and their sink. For an analogous myth cf. BU. 1. 2. 5: "Whatever He (Death, Prajāpati, the Year, the Sun, who is also the Breath of Life) brought forth, that he began to eat".

[8] In all these positions Plato is so closely followed by Plotinus (who ought much rather to be called a Platonist than a "Neo-" Platonist) that I have not thought it necessary to quote him here. An admirable summary of Plotinus on "Time

these are all parts of time; even as 'was' and 'shall be' are generated parts of time, though we casually misapply them to the Eternal Essence [when we call it 'everlasting'],—for we say that Eternity 'is', 'was' and 'shall be', although in truth of speech the 'is' alone is appropriate, while 'was' and 'will be' are properly applicable only to the becoming that proceeds in time, since both are movements; but it does not pertain to that which is always (ἀεί) self-accordant and motionless, to become older or younger by way of time, nor to 'have become so', nor to 'be' so now, nor to be 'about to be so' in the future, nor, in general to be subject to any of the conditions that are associated with what is sensible because of its 'becoming',—these being generated forms of time, which imitates Eternity and revolves according to number. Nor is it really accurate to say of what has become that it 'is' become, or of what becomes that it 'is' becoming, or of what will become that it 'is' about to become, or of the non-existent (τὸ μὴ ὄν) that it 'is' non-existent...[9].

---

and Eternity" will be found in Dean Inge, *The Philosophy of Plotinus,* 2nd ed. 1923, 2. 92-103. Incidentally, the Dean remarks that "the kind of immortality which 'psychical research' endeavours to establish would be for him [Plotinus] a negation of the only immortality which he desires and believes in... Nor does Neoplatonism encourage the belief that the blessed life is a state which will only begin for the individual when the earthly course of the whole human race has reached its term". It has often, indeed, been recognized that Plotinus' position is thoroughly Indian; it by no means follows that he derived many, or any, parts of his doctrine from India.

[9] The like ideas find expression even today, but in the lang-

"Time, then, became together with the Heaven (Universe), so that having been generated together they might also be dissolved together, if ever any dissolution of them should be; and it was made according to the paradigm of the Everlasting (διαιώνια) Nature, to be as much like it as was possible; for while the paradigm 'is' for all Eternity (πάντα αἰῶνά), the copy, on the other hand 'is' for all time (ἅπαντα χρόνον)[10] wholly

---

uage of the time. For example, Wilbur Urban, *The Intelligible World,* 1929, pp. 417-421: "The identification of being with that which becomes, with processes of evolution and devolution is impossible... There is no entropy of being... the two phenomenal categories of life and death [i.e. future and past] are moments in a larger life". That is as much as to say that *being* neither lives nor dies, and that nothing can be added to or subtracted from it; and that as in ŚB. 10. 5. 2. 13 our very *life* depends upon the presence of death within us,—it is one and the same Father who "killeth and maketh alive" (AV. 8. 3. 3; I Sam. 2. 6), one Death who both devours his children and generates them (PB. 21. 2. 1). Wilbur Urban's "terminus" [*a quo* and *ad quem*] corresponds to Aristotle's "moment" or "point" that as its "limit" defines and gives a meaning to existences; and it is not without good reason that Terminus (Hermes) was once a nomen Dei, who is, indeed, at once both man's beginning and his end.

On the other hand, a "scientific" author, J. B. S. Haldane, can write on "Time and Eternity" (in the *Rationalist Annual* for 1946) without for a moment suspecting that he is only discussing time and completely ignoring the traditional meaning of "Eternity"!

[10] In *Meno* 85, 86 the "recollection" of things not learnt in this life is taken to show that the Soul must have existed "throughout all time" and is therefore immortal,—i.e. eternal (ἀΐδια) and imperishable, *Phaedo* 106 D, E; but this argument

such as to have become, exist, and be about to exist", *Timaeus* 29 A, B, and 37 D—38 C.

The same distinctions are implicit in the *Cratylus* 439 E, where it is asked: "How can that which is never self-same 'be' anything? For if it is ever self-same, it is evidently not at that time transient, and if it is always self-same and 'itself', how can it ever change or move without relinquishing its own form?" (*ἡ αὑτοῦ ἰδέα*, exactly Skr. *sva-rūpa*)[11].

Eternity was referred to above as self-same "in Unity" and can hardly be other than the "One" of

---

from pre-existence (and repeated incarnation) is not a rigorous proof, because incarnation itself is a kind of dying, *Phaedo* 95 C, D, cf. JUB. 3. 9. 1 and 4. 9, and St. Bernard, *De grad. humilitatis* 1. 30, Nascimur morituri: ideoque nascimur morituri, quia primus morimur nascituri, and also the various Brahmanical and Buddhist contexts in which it is emphasized that immortality and birth are incompatible, and that the seeds of death are born with us. Cf. St. Augustine, Sermo (*de Scrip. N. T.*) 97. 3. 3, "From the moment a man is born, it may be said, 'He will not get over it'".

[11] This is the predicament of the positivist or "nothing-morist" (*nāstika*), that in acknowledging the reality only of that which can be grasped, he is attributing "reality" to things that cannot be grasped because they never stop to be, and is driven, in spite of himself, to postulate the reality of some such abstract entity as "Energy",—a word that is nothing but one of the names of God. As Wilbur Urban (*Language and Reality*, p. 708) remarks, "the scientist speaks of 'a machine that winds its own springs', therefore of a machine that is not a machine; of a 'natural selection' which is really not a selection",—and in so far as he resorts to these antinomies, abandons logic! "A machine that winds its own springs is as much a fiction as a thinking reed" (*ib.* p. 515).

which the nature is discussed at great length in the *Parmenides* 141 ff. where it is asked whether it "is" or "is not" and how the answer bears upon the nature of the "others". The answers describe the two contrasted natures of one and the same essence; at the same time they remind us very strongly of the Buddhist answers to the question, whether it can be said that an Arahant, after death, "is" or "is not", and of the attribution both of temporality and of timelessness to the Dhamma, and of the distinction of a Nibbāna with or without residual "assumptions". The One is both one and many, and neither one nor many; it both partakes and does not partake of time; it is and is not, changes and does not change. However, if it is, "it is all things and nothing at all"[12]. Now, that it is both unchangeable and also changes, both static and in motion means that "it must itself be *in no time at all*... (for) there is no *time* in which anything can be at once static and in motion... When, then, does it change?... Is there this out-of-place-thing (ἄτοπον)[13] wherein it might be,

---

[12] A significant formula that often recurs in the sayings of the Western "mystics" e.g. in *The Cloud of Unknowing:* "Let be this everywhere and this aught, in comparison of this nowhere and this naught... What is he that calleth it 'naught'? Surely it is our outer man, and not our inner. Our inner man calleth it 'All'... And therefore travail fast (earnestly) in this naught and this nowhere" (cc. 65, 70); and Jacob Boehme: "Nothing and All, or that nothing-visible out of which all things proceed... Whosoever finds it, finds nothing and all things".

[13] Ἄτοπος, rendered usually to be by "extraordinary", but here especially appropriate in its literal sense of "placeless",

'when' it changes? And of what sort? The moment (ἐξαίφνης)[14]! For the moment seems to signify a something from which there is change in both directions... there is this instantaneous nature that has no place (ἄτοπος), something enthroned between motion and stasis, not existent in any time; and it is into this and out of this that whatever is in motion changes to be static[15], and that whatever is static changes to be in motion... But in changing, it changes instantaneously, and not in any time, but when it is neither in motion nor static; and in the same way as regards its other 'changes', as from non-existence (τὸ μὴ εἶναι = *prag-abhāva)*[16] to becoming (τὸ γίγνεσθαι = *bhava)*, from

---

whatever is "not in any time" being necessarily also "not in any place". In Skr. *akāla*, "untimely" is used where in Gk. ἄτοπος, "out of place", would be said.

[14] Here unquestionably "instant" or "moment" without duration, since it is synonymous with "not in any time". Ἐξαίφνης is defined by Aristotle (*Phys.* 4. 13. 222 b) as "minimally removed (from the indivisible now) by an imperceptible time"; in NT. the word is rendered by "suddenly"—Mark 13. 36, Luke 2. 13, 13. 9, Acts 9. 3, 22. 6, and similarly Mark 9. 8 (ἐξάπινα) and Acts 2. 2 (ἄφνω); cf. St. Thomas Aquinas *Sum. Theol.* I-II. 113. 7 on the "suddenness" of the Holy Ghost, and also Plato, *Ep.* 7. 341 C. The word itself seems to mean "out of the unseen" (ἐξ-ἀφανής), while "sudden" means "going stealthily" (*sub-it-aneus*), cf. ἄφνω in the sense of "unawares".

[15] "Static", to be distinguished from "at rest" in the merely relative and physical sense in which things "at rest" are really only in "unstable equilibrium".

[16] Plato's four kinds of non-existence,—the "not yet" of things that may or will exist; the "no longer" (μηκέτι) of things that change and perish so as to "not be" what they

being one to being many, from being like (itself) to being unlike, from being small to being great, and conversely,—so that it is neither in a state of increase nor of decrease nor of equality"[17] (*Parmenides* 147-157 A). so that their participation is both in the Whole (of .Further, it is shown that the "others" participate in the One, but are not parts of it, for it has no parts;

were (like Cleinias, when he changes from being ignorant to being wise, *Euthydemus* 282 D); the "mutual" or "relative" (reference 3 in the text above, and also *Parmenides* 163 C, "absence of existence in which we say that it is not there", and *Sophist* 258 E "as regards others"); and "absolute" (*Parmenides* 163 C "non-existent in any way, shape, or manner", and *Sophist* 237 B τὸ μηδαμῶς ὄν), are respectively identical with the Indian set of four kinds of non-existence, viz. in the same order, *prāgabhāva, pradhvaṁsābhāva, anyonyābhāva,* and *atyantābhāva*. Plato's discussions of non-existence will be found easier to follow if at every point we pause to consider which of the four kinds of non-existence is referred to: whether, for example, πρὸς ἄλληλα (*anyonya*), or μηδαμῶς (*atyanta*); otherwise, the discussion is indefinite, because μή and οὔ always imply a difference of some kind (*Sophist* 257 B, C) and non-existence is not the opposite of existence, but only to be contrasted with it, for there is no "opposite of being" (*ib.* 258 E),—just as the finite is not the opposite of the infinite, but only, so to speak, an excerpt from it. In the non-existent is "that which is uncharacterised" (*yad vai nāsti tad alakṣaṇam,* ŚB. 7. 2. 1. 7); this is *anyonya-* in that it means freedom from affirmative limitations; so that when the Deity is described as *sad-asat* this is tantamount to *niruktāniruktam* and means that it is both with and without such definitions, or in other words both God and Godhead, the Godhead being uncharacterised and so, as Western mystics express it "free in its non-existence", and properly to be called "nihil".

[17] I.e. past, future and present conditions of becoming

which they are parts) and in the One, and it results for these others than the One "because of what they have in common with the One and with themselves, both that there are differences amongst themselves by which they are limited in their relation to one another and to the Whole[18], and that 'their own authentic nature' (ἡ δ' ἑαυτῶν φύσις καθ' ἑαυτά) is unlimited. So that the things that are other than the One, whether as wholes or parts, are both unlimited and participant in limitation" (*ib.* 158 D). In other words, they bear within themselves the "trace" of the One's one-and-manyness, mortality and immortality, etc., being mortal as they are in themselves (ἐν ἑαυτοῖς) and immortal as regards their Selves (καθ' ἑαυτά)[19], which last are their portion in and of the One in its "own form",—a distinction of the "man" from the "Inner man" (ὁ ἐντὸς ἄνθρωπος, *Rep.* 589 B = *ayam antaḥ puruṣaḥ*, CU. 3. 12. 8) that, as in II Cor. 4. 16[20] corresponds exactly to the Indian distinction of the corporeal or elemental self (*śarīra-* or *bhūta-ātman*) from the unborn, indivisible Ultimate Self (*parama-ātman*), the Self of all things-become" (*sarva-bhūtānām ātman*)[21].

The distinction of things as they are "in themselves" from what is "their own authentic nature" (as above,

---

[18] See in Note 1.

[19] "That which is the real self of each of us, and which we term the immortal soul" (*Laws* 959 B, tr. R. G. Bury). Cf. Luke 15. 17 εἰς ἑαυτὸν δὲ ἐλθών.

[20] Cf. II Cor. 4. 16 ὁ ἔξω ἡμῶν ἄνθρωπος διαφθείρεται, ἀλλ' ὁ ἔσω ἡμῶν ἀνακαινοῦταί ἡμέρᾳ καὶ ἡμέρᾳ.

[21] Jacob Boehme's "Being of all beings", passim.

and cf. Sophokles, *Philoctetes* 902, 903 contrasting man's "authentic nature", τὴν αὑτοῦ φύσιν with the "man", ἀνήρ) is further clarified in terms of time and eternity in the *Philebus,* 53 D-59 A: "There are [in our existence] two things, one authentic Self (αὐτὸ καθ' αὑτό), and the other ever pursuing something other than itself... one that is ever for the sake (ἕνεκα) of the things-that-really-are, the other that which having become for the sake of (χάριν, perhaps 'for the love of') the former—(that is) for the sake of something (other than itself)—is ever becoming... (this last) being the becoming (γένεσις, *bhava*)[22] of all things, and the other their essence (οὐσία, *bhāva*)... The truest knowledge (γνῶσις, *jñāna*) is of that which is, and really is, and that is ever natured in accordance with itself (κατὰ ταὐτὸν ἀεὶ πεφυκός[23] = *svayambhū*, in later Gk. αὐτογενής);.. but the technologists are not, as they imagine, students of this Nature (φύσις); what they spend their lives in the investigation of is the things of this world, how they become, what their passion is[24], and how they operate... taking no pains whatever to discover the

[22] Which becoming is inseparable from its opposite, destruction (τὸ φθείρεσθαι), and both of these conditions are other than that third (Middle) and contemplative life in which there is neither gree nor grief, *ib.* 55 A.

[23] Cf. τὸ αὐτοφυές, *Rep.* 486 E; Skr. *svaruḥ*, growing from its own roots: and contrast ἑτεροφυής, "parasitic".

[24] Literally, "how they suffer this or that" (ὅπῃ πάσχει τι), i.e. as we should say, "how they are economically, or otherwise, determined". On the other hand, as Aristotle points out, things not in time are impassible (οὐδὲ πάσχει), change being impossible in that which has no parts (*Phys.* 4. 12. 221 B + 6. 10. 240 B).

things-that-really-are, but only those that become and will become and have become",—temporalia!

For Aristotle, "things eternal (τὰ δ' ἀΐδια) are neither generated nor destroyed" (*Nich. Eth.* 6. 3. 2): "eternal entities (τὰ ἀεὶ ὄντα), by the fact of their eternity, are not in time... the mark of which is their impassibility ... In time all things are generated and destroyed... Time is made up only of the past and the future... the Now is not a part of time at all... Time cannot be divided into atomic parts" (*Phys.* 4. 12, 221 B + 13, 222 B + 10, 218 A + 8. 8, 263 B): and this is as much as to say that Eternity is Now, or not at all.

By the "now that is not a part of time" is meant, of course, the "atomic now" (ἄτομος νῦν) that marks the beginning or the end of any period of time, which end is also the beginning of another period of time, "for time is always in the beginning" (ἀεὶ ἐν ἀρχῇ, *Phys.* 4. 13, 222 B), and like movement, everlasting; or that, in other words, divides the past from the future. So the indivisible Now has the double function of dividing and uniting (ἡ διαίρεσις καὶ ἡ ἕνωσις)[25], and in these two functions is altogether like the undimensioned Point (στιγμή)[26] that simultaneously divides and

[25] "What we have called the Great Person (*mahāpuruṣa*) is the Year that scatters some things and unifies others", i.e. generates some in their diversity and puts an end to the existence of others (AA. 3. 2. 3): *pradhvaṁsayan,* not here "destroys" (empirically) but rather literally "makes dust of" in the sense that "dust thou art" (Gen. 3. 19), and *aikyā bhāvayan,* "slays", cf. BU. 4. 4. 2 *ekī bhavati,* "is dying".

[26] "Point" can be said either with respect to time or space: cf. Plutarch, *Mor.* 117 E "the longest life is short and mo-

unites the parts of a line. As dividers, nows are always differentiated (ἀεὶ ἕτερον) by their relation to different pasts and futures, but as uniters always the same (ᾗ συνδεῖ, ἀεὶ τὸ αὐτό); just as in the case of points which as dividers are manifold (since a line can be divided in different places), but in the sense that the point is that which traces the undivided line, are "the same throughout" (*ib.* 222 A). "Nows", in other words, are all the same, but apparently differentiated by the really different times with which they are associated (*Phys.* 4. 11, 219 B); and that is just as, in terms of transmigration, the *one* "atomic Self" (*aṇur ātman*, Muṇḍ. Up. cited above) is empirically many by the superimposition of the empirical qualities of the many vehicles to which it is present, though it is really always the same and never discontinuous with itself; or to take a different example, just as space is unlimited but apparently differentiated by the boundaries of a

mentary (στιγμαῖος) compared to limitless Eternity", and Dante, *Paradiso* 17. 17 il *punto* a cui tutti li tempi son presenti, "the moment to which all times are present", and 33. 94 un *punto* solo, "a single moment".

The "point (of Time impartite) to which all times are present", and "from which point heaven and the whole of nature depend" (*Paradiso* 28. 41, cf. 13. 11 with RV. 1. 35. 6) is equally the motionless centre of all existence,—"Daz ist der zirkel, den diu sêle umbeloufen hat"—and when the soul has been her rounds and found the circle endless, then she casts herself into the centre, "in ein *punt*" (Meister Eckhart, Pfeiffer 503).

[27] In this paragraph, bracketed numbers refer to E. R. Goodenough, "A Neo-Pythagorean Source in Philo Judaeus", *Yale Classical Studies* III, 1932, pp. 117-164.

jar, but when the jar is broken the "space in which it was" is no longer identifiable. It is interesting that this last illustration is also used by Aristotle himself in *Phys.* 4. 4, 211 B, where he points out that if the imaginary spatial entity left behind when the vessel is removed were really identifiable, this would imply the existence of an infinite number of individual "places" existent in one and the same continuous space.

Here, in parenthesis, it may be observed that the dual functions of the instantaneous now or undimensioned point which divides and unites extents of time or space are precisely *logical* functions, and are, in fact the functions of *the* Logos that is at once the Divider (*τομεύς*) and Unifying Bond (*δεσμός*) of all things, notably as envisaged by Philo, who, starting from Gen. 15. 10 "He divided them in the middle, and laid the pieces opposite each other", describes the created world "as consisting of an almost infinite series of opposites [*ἐναντία*, *dvandvau*] held together in harmony by the very creative impulse or agent which had originally separated them out from primitive and unformed matter by a series of bisections" (132)[27], i.e. de-limitations or measurements[28]. Just as for Heracleitus "reality is a *ἁρμονία* of opposite tensions, a single nature which develops itself in the twofold

[28] It is, perhaps, hardly necessary to say that the concept is referable to Plato, that "God is always geometrizing" (as we see Him in Blake's Ancient of Days, leaning out of the Sun, extending his compasses, cf. RV. 5. 85. 5 *māneneva tasthivān antarikṣe vi yo mame pṛthivīṁ sūryeṇa*, cf. 8. 25. 18 and TS. 5. 4. 6. 5).

directions" (132), so for Philo the "Monad [Plato's 'One' as distinct from the 'others'] is not a number at all, but a premise (στοιχεῖον) and a principle" (ἀρχή, *Heres* 190,—and as such, of course, "ungenerated and indestructible" and "without beginning or end" Plato, *Phaedrus* 245 D + Aristotle, *Phys*. 8.1, 252 B, cf. 3.4. 203 B). "The Monad is the image of God who is single in his unity and at the same time a pleroma", while "the *others*... are held together (σφίγγεται)[29] by the Divine Word" (*Heres* 187, 188),—and so, "the Logos as being God in relation to the world... is at once the Cutter of the universe and the glue binding it together" (133, 146). This "One" (τὸ γὰρ ἕν) is represented by the central light of the sevenfold λυχνία, of which the *golden*[30] material is the symbol of unbreakable extensibility and so of total presence (*Heres* 215f.)[31], while elsewhere the characteristic symbol of the Logos is the Pillar, i.e. Axis Mundi.

It is emphasized by Philo (*Heres* 207 f. and passim), and recognized throughout the tradition, what is obvious enough, that all *creation* and *existence* involves a distinction or separation of contrary concepts; nothing

---

[29] I cannot here enlarge upon values of σφίγγω and Σφίγξ, except to say that the Sphinx is certainly not "the strangler", but much rather (as Clement of Alexandria also saw) "the bond" that holds the universe together.

[30] Gold, as in India, passim, being the recognized symbol of life, light, truth, and immortality.

[31] Compare Daqīqī's wonderful vision of the seven candles that become one, and that are also seven men, and seven trees that are both seven and one, Rūmī, *Mathnawī* 3. 1985ff.

that was or will be, or that is "now" in the vaguer sense of the word, but is qualitatively "this" and "not that". So it is that for Nicolas of Cusa (*De vis. Dei* c. IX) it is of these contraries that the wall of Paradise, wherein God dwells, is built, and no one who has not overcome "the highest spirit of reason" [i.e. the Logos] that guards the undimensioned point that divides the contraries from one another and unites them can attain to the coincidence of opposites that subsists in the divine intellect: and in the same way in India, Liberation is "from the delusion of the pairs" (*dvandva-moha-nirmuktāḥ* BG. 7. 28, *dvandvātito . . . na nibadhyate,* 4. 22), "overcoming the pairs" (MU. 3. 1). It is inasmuch as "strait is the gate and narrow is the way that leadeth unto life" that "few there be that find it" (Math. 7. 14): "I am the door" (John 10. 9); "Now (νῦν) is the day of salvation"... In a moment (ἐν ἀτόμῳ), the twinkling of an eye, we shall be changed" (II Cor. 6. 2 and I Cor. 15. 52). In other words, our op*port*unity is instantaneous, and this is apparent in all the traditional accounts of the passage of the Symplegades or Sundoor, whether Greek, Irish, American or Indian[31a]; for example in the *Mahābhārata* (Poona ed. I. 29. 4) where the "Active Door" is an ever revolving razor-edged wheel (as in Genesis "a flaming sword which turned every way") between the spokes of which "the Skyfarer, diminishing his body, darted in an instant" (*kṣaṇena*), — that very "moment without duration", of

[31a] See my "Symplegades" in M. F. Ashley Montagu (Ed.), *Studies . . . Offered in Homage to George Sarton . . .,* 1947.

which we have been speaking, and "apart from which there is no side door here in the world".

In connection with the "door" one further point should be noted; in actual walls, doors are not necessarily median, but may be near or far from one or the other end of the wall, just as a line can be bisected not only in the middle, but anywhere: whereas Philo emphasizes that the logical Divider and Uniter is always in the middle and always makes divisions of two exactly equal parts. All that this apparent discrepancy means is that actual walls or lines are artificially delimited from a potentially indefinite extension in either direction, and that the position of the door or point is accidental. Whereas, if we think of the opposites, simply as past and future, or as extents on this or that side of a dividing point, the two parts are exactly equal in extent because both extents are indefinite and unlimited, and this will be true wherever the dividing point may be accidentally placed. It is precisely for this reason that in some versions of the myth of the Symplegades, the Hero, seeking to avoid the dangerous passage of the clashing opposites, is said to turn aside in each direction, trying to find a way around the barriers, but has to abandon such an endless quest, and return to the "point" of division and contact; for, indeed, he will find no other passage than that which is afforded by this point that retains its median position all down the line, wherever it may be, and than which Via Media there is no other Way. It is only by approaching the murity at right angles, that is to say along the Axis Mundi or Seventh Ray, that one can hope to pass "through the midst of the Sun"; the Way is just as narrow as the Gate is strait.

To return to Aristotle; in discussing the essential identity of the indivisible Now, and the accidental distinction of the two Nows that delimit a given period of time he says, with reference to their difference that "if simultaneity as to time, and not being before or after, implies coincidence, and is in the Now, if the before and after are both in one and the same Now, then what happened ten thousand years ago would be simultaneous with what is happening today, and nothing would be before or after anything else" (*Phys.* 4. 10, 218 A). Again, whether One or accidentally two, the Now itself is not in time so as to be a part of it, but only in the sense that time surrounds it, much as the sea surrounds an island. Were the Now in time as a part is *in* a whole, "then everything would be in anything, and the universe in a grain of millet, only because the grain of millet and the universe are both existent at the same time" (*ib.* 4. 12, 221 A). It seems to me that the only purpose of these difficult statements is to distinguish the accidental simultaneity of things in time from their essential simultaneity apart from time, in the Now that unites the past and the future; and that it must be the whole of the past and the future, in neither of which is there any discontinuity, that meet in the Now that faces both ways. Aristotle can hardly have meant to deny the simultaneity of past and future in this One and Eternal Now, or to deny that there is a sense in which the universe is "in a grain of millet"; for if the grain and the universe are considered not in their extension but as regards their common and immutable essence that insists in the absolute Now, then it can be said that the universe is "in" the grain at the same time that the grain is in the universe,—in the words of William Blake, "a World in a grain of sand, and Eternity in an hour".

I do not propose to cite these doctrines in detail as they recur in the works of the Hermetists and Neoplatonists. I must, however, quote from "Hermes Trismegistos" a passage at once Platonic and Aristotelian, and one might say also "Indian":

"All things on earth are overtaken by destruction (*φθορά*); for without destruction there can be no origination (*γένεσις*). The things that come into being must needs arise from those that are destroyed; and those that come into being must be destroyed, if origination (or 'becoming') is to go on. But the things that come into being out of destruction must be false (*ψεῦδος*) [32], because they become different at different times. For it is impossible for the same things to become a second time; and how can that be real (or 'true') which is not the same that it was before,... Man himself, insofar as he is a man, is not real. For the real is that which is absolutely self-subsistent, and remains what it is in itself; but man is a composite of many things, and does not remain such as he is in himself, but shifts

[32] "False", but not necessarily deceptive, unless by our own fault we suppose that all *is* gold that glitters. An imitation is not unreal as such, but is not the reality of which it is an imitation.

and changes from one age to another, and from one form (ἰδέα) to another. Oftentimes men fail to recognize their own children after a short interval, and children likewise fail to recognize their parents... You must understand that that alone that ever *is,* is real. But a man is not a thing that ever is... nothing is real that does not remain what it is... The [Supernal] Sun, who does not change, but remains what he is, is real... He rules over all things, and makes all things; him do I worship, and I adore his Truth, acknowledging him as the Maker, next after the Primal One[33]. What then, is the Primal Truth (or Reality)? Only that One, who is not made of matter, nor embodied, who is colourless and formless, changeless and unalterable; and who Is eternally"[34].

---

[33] I cannot agree with Scott that the passage referring to the Sun "is inconsistent with the text; the reference is not to the physical sun, but to the intelligible Sun, and Scott is falling into the error derided by Plutarch, that of confusing Helios with Apollo even when the word Helios really stands for Apollo. Cf. my note 7 in *Psychiatry* 8, 1945, p. 288, and the distinction, throughout tradition, of the sensible from the spiritual Sun. Put into Christian terms, all that Hermes is saying is that both the Son ("through whom all things were made") and the Father are "true" or "real", but the latter even more superlatively so.

[34] Scott, *Hermetica* 1.387-389 (Excerpt II A, Hermes to Tat). The last sentence might have been taken word for word from an Upanishad (e.g. KU. 3. 15), as a description of Brahma, That One.

Hermes (whom Plutarch and Hippolytus identified with "Reason") also discusses "the three times" and remarks that "they are made one by their continuity; but "seeing that the

Plutarch, who may not be very "original", but is a very good philosopher, quotes Heracleitus and goes on: "nor is it possible to lay hold twice of any mortal substance in the same state; by the sharpness and swiftness of the change in it there 'comes dispersion and again combination'; or, rather, not at another time nor later, but *at the same instant* (ἅμα) it both takes its place and leaves it and 'comes and goes'. So that that which is born of it never attains to being... Dead is the man of yesterday, for he has died into the man of today (σήμερον = Skr. *sadya*) ... No one persists, nor is he 'one', but becomes many... and if he changes, he is not the same, and if he is not the same, he is not 'himself', but himself changes as other proceeds from other. Our sensibility, through ignorance of what really is, falsely tells that the appearance 'is'.

"What, then, is that which really is? That which is eternal, unborn and unperishing, and to which time brings no change. For time is something moving, apparent in connection with matter in motion, ever

---

present does not stand fast, even for an instant (κέντρον = *punctus*), how can it be said to *be* 'present' (lit. 'in-standing') when it cannot stand in equilibrium?" (ῥοπή) (Excerpt 10); and "that which is ever becoming is ever perishing, but that which has become once for all (ἅπαξ) perishes not at all" (Excerpt 11, 5). All this is equally Aristotelian and Buddhist. The last corresponds exactly to BG. 2. 20 b, "nor having come to be, will he ever more come not to be"; any supposed objection to such an expression as "having come to be" falling away because the reference is really to That One who is "self-become" (*svayam-bhū*, αὐτοφυής) and was not *brought* into being by any external cause. Cf. *infra*, p. 65, l. 1.

flowing (ῥέον ἀεί), not a retainer, but as it were a vessel of destruction and becoming, whose familiar 'after' and 'before', 'shall be' and 'has been' when they are said, are of themselves a confession of not being... For 'now' is crowded out into the future and the past, when we regard it as a point [of time]; for of necessity it suffers a division [is not an ἄτομος νῦν].

"But, it hardly need be said, God *is*, and He is not for any time but for the eternity (αἰών) that is motionless and timeless and undeviating, and wherein there is no before nor after, nor future nor past, nor older nor younger; but He, being One, has with one [indivisible] 'Now' filled 'for ever'"[35].

Finally, for Plotinus (*Enneads* 2. 4. 7 and 3. 7. 3-11), for whom "there are no atoms; all body is divisible endlessly", time and motion are continuous; and time, an imitation of Eternity, is "the life of the soul as she passes from one phase of activity or experience to another". On the other hand, Eternity, in the last analysis identical with God, "is a life changelessly motionless and ever holding the universal content in actual presence; not this now and now that other, but always all... self-same, for ever in the present Now... whole, in the full sense that nothing whatever is absent from it. So that nothing is in store for it: for if any-

---

[35] Plutarch, *Moralia* 392 C-393 A. In 422 C he speaks also of eternity" "whence time, like an ever-flowing stream, is conveyed to the worlds as being "round about" (πέρι) all things, i.e. all-pervading. In another sense, of course, all things are "round about" eternity, as the circumference surrounds the centre. Cf. St. Augustine, infra, p. 106, n. 4.

thing were yet to come, that thing must have been lacking to it, and so it could not be the All. ... The word, Eternity (αἰών), itself means 'ever-being' (ἀεὶ ὄν). ... though 'always', spoken not of time but of the incorruptible and endlessly whole, is liable to introduce the false notions of stage or interval ... it were better to say 'Being' simply, since 'everlasting' really adds nothing to the concept of Being ... which has no connection with any quantity, such as instalments of time, but *is* prior to all quantity ... Life, instantaneously entire, complete, nowhere broken into period or part, pertaining to the Self-existent by the very fact that it *is*, that has been the object of our enquiry, that is Eternity". And he adds that motion, the circling of all things round about their eternal centre, "is their seeking after perpetuity by way of futurity". After Plotinus, we reach the beginning of the Middle Ages, with St. Augustine and Boethius, in whom the Platonic tradition persists.

IV

ISLĀM

D. B. Macdonald has dealt with a part of our subject at some length in *Isis* 30 (June 1927), in an article entitled "Continuous re-creation and atomic time in Muslim scholastic theology". He starts with Maimonides' account of Muslim "atomism"; according to which, he says, the world is made of atoms that "have no quantity, but out of which compounds can be made which possess quantity" and that exist in a vacuum; that is, there is a separation between them in which absolutely nothing, body or atom, exists... Time is made up of now's (*'ānāt*) [1]... This means that time is made up of a great many 'times' which cannot be further subdivided... Accidents are inseparable from the atoms... the accident does not last two atoms of time. This means that when Allah creates a material atom he creates in it whatever accidents he wills... When an accident is created it passes away at once; then Allah creates another accident of the

[1] As Macdonald himself points out, this is *not* the Aristotelian doctrine but, rather, "based on the paradoxes of Zeno, which cannot be logically resolved except by eliminating all infinitesimals". It may have been the Ash'arite doctrine, but is certainly not that of the indivisible "instant" of the Ṣūfīs.

same kind ... he is absolutely the only agent [*aslī kār*] in existence... [but] he creates in the mind of the supposed actor an 'accepting as his own' of his supposed act[2]... Only Allah... holds together the

---

[2] The notion that "I am the agent" is fallacious equally from the Islamic, Vedantic and Buddhist points of view, and for Philo, whose *οἴησις* = Skr. and Pali *māna,* all with reference to the egocentric delusions, "*I* do", "*I* am", etc. This by no means relieves the "individual" of full responsibility for "his" actions; injunctions and prohibitions are valid for him, and he will reap as he sows, for so long as his individuality lasts.

In Islam, the "necessitarianism" (*jabr*) that would make of man a merely passive instrument is a well recognized heresy (for some of the references see Nicholson, *Mathnawī,* Commentary 1. 45, and s.v. "necessitarianism" and *jabr* in the Index). So also in Hinduism and Buddhism, where the notion that "I am the agent" is equally fallacious, it is God alone who acts in us, but this in no way relieves the man of responsibility for so long as as he still thinks of himself as "this man, So-and-so", and it is a heresy to maintain that there is no "ought to be done" and "ought not to be done"; freedom from obligation is only for those who are no longer anyone. All injunctions and prohibitions imply a freewill attributed to those to whom they apply. For some of the references see Śaṅkarācārya, BrSBh. 2. 3. 48 (SBE. 38. 66) and s. vv. *Akiriyavāda* and *Ahaṁkāra* in HJAS. 4, 1939, pp. 119, 129.

The Christian position is not different. If it holds for Christ that "I do nothing of myself... the Father that dwelleth in me, he doeth the works" (John 8. 28; 14. 10) it is hardly for his followers to assert their own independent agency, but only to be, like their exemplar, "co-workers with Him who doeth the works" (St. Augustine, *De nat. et gratia* 31. 35). Man, of himself, merely behaves ill or well, and is under the Law. But "if ye be led of the Spirit, ye are not under the law" (Gal.

whole stream of the existence of the world... Allah is the only Reality... We must eliminate the conception of causality from the universe except as to the imme-

---

5. 18), "whoever is born of God cannot sin" (1 John 3. 9); "the acts of a man who is led by the Holy Ghost are not his acts, but those of the Holy Ghost" (St. Th. Aquinas, *Sum. Theol.* I-II. 96. 2 ad 3). The same applies to lies and truth; man in himself is a liar (Ps. 115. 11; John 8. 44; St. Augustine, *Sermo [De Script N.T.]* 166. 2. 2 and 3. 3; cf. Heracleitus as interpreted by Sextus Empiricus *ΠΡΟΣ ΛΟΓΙΚΟΥΣ* 131-134), but "all that is true, by whomsoever it has been said, is from the Holy Ghost" (St. Ambrose on 1 Cor. 12. 3).

All this can only be rightly understood when the nature of an *act*, and the relation of act to being has been rightly understood. No sin is an "act", but only a failure to act, as the words mis-deed, Un-that, *akṛtam* truly tell us. Sinners themselves, "insofar as they are sinners, have no being at all, but fall short of it" (St. Th. Aquinas, *Sum. Theol.* 1. 20. 2 ad 4): that is, not being "in act", are not "in being". Accordingly, whatever is "not-done", every mis-deed, is referable to man as he is in himself, a virtual non-entity, but whatever is really *done* is referable to God, and so He is the "sole agent".

Freewill is not a liberty to do as one likes—a matter of passive reaction to pleasure and pain, and anything but a freedom. Freewill is the liberty to accept or refuse the status of "co-workers with God", to appropriate or shirk the specific functions that have been delegated to men as vocations ("for everyone is predisposed by God to that for which he was created", Ḥadīth), and to obey or disobey the Natural Law. The human puppet is free to hold or not hold onto the "golden cord" (of the "thread-spirit") and either acts or merely reacts accordingly (Plato, *Laws* 644). "To 'act' (*facere*) and suffer belongs to bodies and their soul; for it both 'acts' in the body and suffers through the body. But truly to act (*facere vero*) belongs only to God and other divine essences" (Boethius, *Contra Eutychen* 1. 1).

diate, moment by moment, working of Allah". Finally (p. 337) he finds in Maimonides' exposition that "motion" seems to our senses to be continuous, but we know by reason that it consists of a series of leaps and rests. The pictures in the cinematograph of re-creation in each successive moment of time produce a continuous impression on our eyes; but it is an illusion, and reason, demonstrating that time must be in atoms, convinces us of that".

Elsewhere [3] Macdonald had remarked of the Muslim atomists that "these atoms of space or time, in either case without extension, are precisely the same as Aristotle's". But this would certainly not be true of the Muslim atoms as described by Maimonides; and while Aristotle's *ἄτομος νῦν* is the same as the Islamic *andar waqt* and Boethius' *nunc stans,* it is equally certain that Aristotle was not himself an atomist in the material sense. Macdonald seems to be quite unaware that his own cinematographic analogy is invalid, in the first place because the successive "frames" are *not* "without extension", and secondly inasmuch as it is precisely "reason"—in this case, actually, Aristotle's "reasoning"—that makes it perfectly clear that time and space are continuous and that motion is anything but "a series of leaps and rests". Macdonald himself does not seem to realise that nothing that *has* extension can be "made of" parts that have none!

Macdonald points out that the Arabic word *jauhar,*

---

[3] D. B. Macdonald, *The Development of Muslim Theology, Jurisprudence, and Constitutional Theory,* New York, 1903, p. 202.

Persian *gauhar,* originally a "gem" of any kind[4], "developed many secondary meanings. In philosophy it has become the broadest word for 'substance', *οὐσία, ens, essentia;* but for the atomistic philosophers it means 'atom' in the exact sense, 'a part which cannot be further parted'. Sometimes they add the word 'separate' (*fard*)... Finally, just like our word 'substance', *jawhar* came to be used for a portion of matter, a physical body". Later on he quotes Ibn Ḥazm (d. 1064, a century and a half before Maimonides), who rejected Ash'arite doctrines and therewith that of "separate atoms" (*al-jauhar al-fard*); and remarks that Ibn Ḥazm's *jauhar* is the Aristotelian "substance", as it seems, indeed, to be. For Ibn Ḥazm, "Allah is perpetually giving existence to every entity, as long as it is an entity, at every moment (*waqt*) of time". Macdonald further remarks that al-Ghazālī, whose influence "triumphed", "seems to have rejected entirely the atomic scheme and to have attached himself to the Aristotelian-Platonic wing".

---

[4] *Gauhar,* accordingly, as "gem" or "pearl", corresponds to Skr. *maṇi,* a word that can be used absolutely in the singular (*Oṁ maṇi padme huṁ;* cf. "Pearl" of great price), and in the plural not only to denote gems or pearls, but philosophically, as in the *sūtrātman* doctrine (BG. 7. 7, etc.), to mean "substances" or "entities". It seems to me that that exactly corresponds to our use of "Being" absolutely, side by side with "beings", which last are, nevertheless, in reality only "becomings", participant in Being; or to the concept of *the* Word, and that of "words" of which the truth depends upon their participation in the truth of that Word in which all things are spoken simultaneously.

be, consulted in Maimonides' *Guide for the Perplexed,* translated by M. Friedlander, 2nd ed., 1925, p.120-144 (i.e. Part 1, ch. lxxiii). Maimonides is by no means describing a doctrine in which he believes, but that of the Muslim Mutakallemim, followers of "The Word" (*al-qalām*), whom one might call fundamentalists; he never refers to the Ṣūfis. Having remarked of the Mutakallemim that they believed in indivisible atoms not only of matter but also of time and space, separated from one another by a vacuum, he very properly remarks that "the Mutakallemim did not at all understand the nature of time" (Third Proposition).

The foregoing is taken from Macdonald's summary in *Isis;* the original in full can be easily, and should be consulted in Maimonides' *Guide for the Perplexed,* translated by M. Friedlander, 2nd ed., 1926, pp. 120—124 (i.e. pt. 1, ch. lxxxiii).

Elsewhere[5] Macdonald remarks that the "ʿIlm al-Kalām [Science of the Word] came to mean not simply theology, but scholastic theology of an atomistic type, going back most strangely to Democritus and Epicurus, and a *mutakallim* came to mean a theologian, at first a Muʿtazilite and later orthodox, behind whose orthodoxy lay the atomistic system that was Islām's most original contribution [!] to theology"[6]. The Mutakallemim, he says, called themselves Ashʿarites. We realise, then, that Maimonides, on whom he (Macdonald) relies, and although he (Maimonides) lived a century

[5] Hasting's *Encyclopaedia of Religion and Ethics,* II. 672, 673.

[6] How so, if derived from Democritus and Epicurus?

later than al-Hujwīrī, is really telling us nothing about the Ṣūfī doctrines of Time and time, of which the affinities are with Aristotle and the Neoplatonists; and that any confusions apparent in Maimonides' account are of little significance for us, whose concern is not with atomism as a physical hypothesis but only with the relation of extended time and traversable space to the Time and Space that are indivisible and unextended. I wonder, indeed, whether Macdonald himself understood the problems involved: for he says, "the division of time into atoms, which could not be further divided ... goes back to Zeno's paradox of Achilles and the tortoise; it was a solution of that paradox, and made motion possible",—whereas it is precisely the theory of *dis*continuous time that makes motion impossible!

In the *Encyclopaedia of Islam*, s. v. Allāh, 1, p. 307, Macdonald quotes from his own *Development of Muslim Theology*, already cited: Of the Ash'arites he says that "when they rejected the Aristotelian view of matter as the possibility of receiving form, their path, of necessity, led them straight to the atomists... Their atoms were not of space only, but of time. The basis of all the manifestations of the world... is a multitude of monads. Each has extension neither in space nor time. They have simply position, not bulk, and do not touch one another. Between them is absolute void. The time-atoms, if the expression may be permitted, are equally unextended and have, also absolute void—of time—between them ... time is only in a succession of untouching moments, and leaps across the void from one to the other with the jerk of the hand of a clock"[7]. Again, "no one [atom] is the cause of the other" and this "annihilates the machinery of the universe", i.e. ignores the operation of mediate causes. From what has been said above, it will be seen how un-Greek this all is, and how irrational; if this was Islām's "most original contribution to theology", it was certainly nothing to be proud of.

At the end of his treatment of the subject in *Isis,* Macdonald proceeds to discuss "the exceedingly difficult question of the origin of this atomic scheme in Islàm". He says that it goes back in its beginnings to Muslim heresy"[8]. By heretics he means "all who applied dialectic to questions of the Faith". But, he asks, "how did the system of material atoms come to be combined with a system of time-atoms and made into a complete theory of the origin of the universe?" He is unable to find "any trace of anything of the kind in Greek thought" and cannot believe "that the Muslim thinkers originated it", although "they were certainly the immediate heirs of the Greek civilization so far as science and philosophy were concerned". He remarks that "the Muslim scientific civilization cannot be explained entirely as a product of Greek influence" and that "there is a tendency at present among students

---

[7] Need it be pointed out that the jerks of the hands of the clock are *not* movements of time? They take place in brief durations of time, which is itself continuous and uninterrupted.

[8] He refers to M. Horten, *Philosophische Systeme der speculativen Theologen im Islam* [date?] and to De Boer's "Atomic Theory (Muhammadan)" in Hasting's *Encyclopaedia of Religion and Ethics.*

of Islam to look to India for a solution of some of our remaining problems". He turns therefore to India, and suggests that the Muslin atomism is derived from Buddhist sources[9].

Now I am not much enamoured of researches into origins or sources undertaken in this historical manner, and prefer simply to recognise the common ground on which the traditions rest, and to regard it as one that belongs to all of them by right of inheritance from antecedent sources ultimately beyond the reach of historical investigation. The question is further complicated by the fact that the Pythagorean-Platonic-Aristotelian philosophies already embody so much that is equally Vedic and Buddhist; the problem of origins thus arising at the very beginning, so to speak, of our studies. If, nevertheless, we are to discuss the affinities of Islamic and Indian philosophy (not forgetting that, as Jahāngir remarked, Vedānta and Taṣawwuf "are the same"), it cannot be overlooked that, for

---

[9] Known to him only from H. Jacobi's "Atomic Theory (Indian)" in Hasting's *Encyclopaedia,* and from S. Dasgupta's *History of Indian Philosophy:* but more fully outlined above, with further references.

I cannot see that the Ashʿarite doctrines could have been derived from Buddhist sources; on the other hand, the Ṣūfī doctrine of the "moment" (*waqt*) could have been so derived, though it does not follow that is was in fact so derived.

[10] On the limitations of the "historical method" cf. René Guénon, *Introduction to the Study of Hindu Doctrines,* 1945, pp. 18, 20, 58, 65, 237, 300. Historical method is only of limited value here, partly because metaphysical doctrines "do not 'evolve' in the Western sense of the word" and partly

instance, R. A. Nicholson overstressed Greek and neglected equally striking equivalences of Ṣūfī with Indian metaphysics. For instance, in Jāmī's *Lawā'ih* XXV the words

> What, seen as relative, appears the world
> Viewed in its essence is the very 'Truth'

imply just what is meant by the Buddhist expression, *yas saṁsāras tan nirvāṇam*, "the flux and the absolute are the same". There are very few metaphysical doctrines in Islam that could not, if one made the attempt, be very plausibly derived from Vedic or Buddhist sources.

But all this is to ignore another side of the question: one that is represented by the survival of the doctrine of the Eternal Now, or *nunc stans*, in Christian philosophy; for example, Meister Eckhart's words, "God is creating the world now, this instant" (Pfeiffer p. 206) might have been said by any Ṣūfī,, but are almost certainly *not* of Buddhist origin. In fact, the whole doctrine of "time and eternity" in Ṣūfī Islamic and Christian contexts could have been derived from Platonic-Aristotelian sources. Not that the question is of great importance: historical studies have a certain value in that the universality of fundamental ideas can be demonstrated as against those who think of them as having been the inventions of these who enunciate

because "in a general way and in most instances a traditional text is no more than a recording, at a relatively recent date, of a teaching which was originally transmitted by word of mouth and to which an author can rarely be assigned".

them; for the rest, the literary history of ideas is of ultimate value only in so far as it can contribute to the answering of the questions, Is such and such a doctrine true, and How can it best be disentangled from individually heretical misinterpretations, and so rightly understood.

We have discussed the atomism of the Mutakallemim at so much length only to dispose of it, and can now consider the Ṣūfī doctrines of time and eternity, of which the expansion must antedate al-Hujwīrī's treatise.

The *Kashf al-Maḥjūb* of al-Hujwīrī (d. 1071-2 A.D.)[11], "the most ancient and celebrated Persian treatise of Ṣūfism" asserts: "Knowledge of 'time' (*waqt*), and of all outward and inward circumstances of which the due effect depends on 'time', is incumbent on everyone" (p. 13). Time has both external and internal aspects, things pertaining to the practise of religion belonging to the former, and true cognition to the latter; but these exoteric and esoteric aspects of Truth must not be divorced" (p. 14),—it is not, in fact, without a full acknowledgement of the truth that "knowledge without action is not knowledge" (p. 12) that the present thesis is restricted to a consideration of "Time" in its absolute and "interior" sense. In this sense, "*waqt* is that whereby a man becomes independent of past and future". Those who possess it say: "we are happy with God in the present (*andar*

[11] The page references are to R. A. Nicholson's version, Gibb Memorial Series XVII, 1st ed. 1911.

waqt). If we occupy ourselves with to-morrow, or let any thought of it enter our minds, we shall be veiled (from God)". Again, "the most precious of human things is the state of being occupied between the past and future... and the Shaykhs have said that 'Time [i.e. Now] is a cutting sword', because it is characteristic of a sword to cut, and 'Time' cuts the roots of the future and the past, and obliterates care of yesterday and tomorrow from the heart" (pp. 368-9)[12]. In other words, Time is the devourer of time,—as in AB. 3. 44 and MU. 6. 2.

The experience of "Time" in this interior sense may be found or lost: "*waqt* has need of *ḥāl* [condition], for *waqt* is beautified by *ḥāl* and subsists thereby[13]. When the owner of *waqt* comes into possession of *ḥāl*, he is no more subject to

---

[12] The foregoing statements imply, of course, that we should "let the dead bury their dead" and "take no thought for the morrow". For Time (the Eternal Now) as "a cutting sword", cf. above, p. 76, on the Lógos Tomeús: as in the Ode from Shams-i-Tabrīz' *Dīwān* translated by Nicholson in *JRAS*. 1913, "The lovely winner of hearts became a sword and appeared in the hand of ʿAlī and became the slayer of time", the immediate allusion being to the sword Dhū'lfiqār given to ʿAlī by the Prophet and that is the death of those who "die before they die"; and that is also the sword of the Word of God that "sunders soul from spirit", Heb. 4. 12. Cf. my "Sir Gawain and the Green Knight", *Speculum* 19. 17 (1944), and Rūmī, *Mathnawī* 6. 1522.

[13] Actually, *ḥāl* as "condition" or "mode" or "ecstasy" implies the experient's real response to the momentary illumination, but not a stability or permanence in the sense that *maqām* is a "station".

change, and is made steadfast (*mustaqim*) in his state... He who is [still] in the state of becoming (*mutakawwin*)[14] may be forgetful, and on him who is thus forgetful *ḥāl* descends and *waqt* is made stable. Thus, Jacob had *waqt*; "now he was blinded by separation, now he was restored to sight by union". But "Abraham was a possessor of *ḥāl*: he was not conscious of separation, that he should be stricken with grief, nor of union, that he should be filled with joy" (pp. 373-4). The "interior Time" is the "instant of illumination" that is so often compared to a flash of lightning; it is only when "the light is constant, and the instant has become all time"[15] that the Sun "never sets"[16].

Jāmī, in the *Lawā'ih* ("Flashes", Clartés), XXVI[17], summarises the doctrine of the Moment (or "interior

[14] *Kaun,* as remarked by D. B. Macdonald, *l. c. supra,* p. 329, is to "become", the infinitive serving for the noun, just as *werden* means "becoming". It would follow that the creative Word *kun* (imp. of *kaun*) is the Command, "Become", and that for the usual rendering "God said, or says, Be, and it was, or is" should be substituted "God said, or says, Become, and it became, or becomes". This would also agree with the meaning of the expressions *dū kaun,* "the two becomings", past and future.

[15] Maurice Browne, *The Atom and the Way,* London, 1946, p. 36. Cf. p. 19, "illumination occurs instantaneously and, for most of us, lasts but a moment. It is by no means momentary, however, for all". Cf. W. Allen, *The Timeless Moment,* London, 1946.

[16] See above, pp. 13, 15.

[17] E. H. Whinfield and M. M. Kazwīnī, *Lawā'ih,* Oriental Translation Fund XVI, London 1906, pp. 42-45.

Time") according to Ibnu'l-'Arabī: "the universe consists of accidents pertaining to a single substance, which is the Reality underlying all existences. This universe is changed and renewed unceasingly at every moment and every breath. Every instant one universe is annihiliated and another resembling it takes its place... In consequence of this rapid succession, the spectator is deceived into the belief that the universe is a permanent existence...

> The being of the world's a wave, it lasts
> One moment, and the next it has to go...
> In the world, men of insight may discern
> A stream whose currents swirl and surge and churn,
> And from the force that works within the stream
> The hidden working of the Truth may learn...[18]

---

[18] Compare the hymn by Isaac Watts (1719):

> A thousand ages in Thy sight
> Are like an evening gone;
> Short as the watch that ends the night
> Before the rising sun.
> Time, like an ever-rolling stream
> Bears all its sons away...

"Before the rising sun": i.e. "Dawn", the instant *saṁdhi* separating and uniting night and day (past and future), called also *brahma-bhūti,* "Theosis". In nearly the same way, Persian *fajr,* ordinarily "daybreak" or "dawn" is also the *nūr-i tajallī,* the Light of the Divine Epiphany (Nicholson, Comment on *Mathnawī* 5. 3309). For a fuller discussion of this meeting-place of Day and Night see my "Symplegades" in M. F. Ashley Montagu *Studies... Offered in Homage to George Sarton,* 1947, p. 463ff., cf. above, p. 23, note 3, and pp. 78-80.

Thus, it never happens that the Very Being is revealed for two successive moments under the guise of the same phenomenon".

R. A. Nicholson similarly summarises Ibnu'l-'Arabī's doctrine: "Phenomena are perpetually changing and being created anew, while God remains as He ever was, is, and shall be. The whole infinite series of individualisations is in fact one eternal and everlasting *tajalli* [illumination] which never repeats itself", adding in a Footnote the important reservation "but there is no moment of not-being between the successive acts of creation", taking this from al-'Arabī, *Fuṣuṣu'-Ḥikam,* 196 f.[19]. Both the *Lawā'ih* and Nicholson emphasize a distinction between the Ibnu'l-'Arabī's true doctrine and that of the Ash'arite "atomists" who seem to have believed in an independent reality of momentary monads, whereas "Ibnu'l-'Arabī will brook no *secundum quid,* not even one that endures only for a moment". Here we seem to meet again with the distinction of a materialist atomism from the very different principle of an atomic time or space without duration or dimensions, and therefore immaterial.

The concept of the absolute and indivisible Time, or Eternity, reappears again in Jalālu'd Dīn Rūmī's magnificent *Mathnawī.* The saying that "this world is but a moment" (*sā'at*) [20] is attributed to the Prophet:

---

[19] R. A. Nicholson, *Studies in Islamic Mysticism,* Cambridge 1921, p. 154.

[20] Cf. *Mathnawī* 3. 2074-2075, "to escape from the moments (*sā'at*) is to escape from change ... When for a moment you escape from the moments, mode is no more". Note also

"Every instant, then, thou art dying and returning... The world is renewed at each breath (*nafas*), and we know it not because it remains (apparently the same). Life is ever arriving anew, like the stream [21], though in the body it has the semblance of continuity: because of its rapidity it seems to be continuous, like the spark that thou revolvest swiftly with thy hand... The swift motion produced by the action of God presents this length of duration [extended time] as [an appearance caused by] the rapidity of the Divine Action" (*Mathnawī* 1.1142-8),—or as a Christian would express it, by the "suddenness" of the Holy Spirit. The analogy is a good one because, in fact, the "spark" that represents the Now of Eternity is unique, whatever its apparent position on the line of *incessant* motion. Nicholson comments: "The whole circle of creation [Skr. *bhava-cakra,* St. James' ὁ τροχὸς τῆς γενέσεως] really begins and ends in a single point, i.e. the Essence of God, which is perceived by us under the form of extension... a flash of Divine illumination (*tajallī*) revealing the One as the Many and the Many as the One".

At the same time, the *Ṣūfī* concept of the momentary existence of accidents (*'arẓ,* i.e. doings, events, happenings, intentions) in no way excludes the continuous operation of causality, linking past with future events. "Were there no translation or recurrence of accidents,

---

as-sā'at, the moment, Resurrection; like the Buddhist *eka-kṣaṇa-sambodhi.*

[21] Cf. Heracleitus frs. 41, 85; the Buddhist stream that "never rests"; St. Augustine's "continuous stream of ever-flowing succession" (*De Trin.* 3. 6).

action would be in vain... But these accidents are transient in another guise; the recurrence of everything mortal is another existence... All the parts of the world are the result of nothing but accident... This is produced by that, and that by this, in productive succession... This world and that are forever giving birth, every cause is a mother, the effect is born as its child; and when the effect was born, that, too, became a cause" (*Mathnawī*, 2.960-1000 [22]). But the operation of this causality is mysterious, "hidden, and not clearly seen" [23].

Again, regarding the man transcending space, in whom is the Light of God; what has *he* to do with the past, or future, or present? "His existence in time past or future is only in relation to you; both are the same to Him, but *you* think them two" (*Mathnawī* 111.1152-3). "Feed me, for I am hungry, and make haste, for 'the Moment (*waqt*) is a cutting sword', and the Ṣufi is a 'son of the Moment' (*ibnu'l waqt*); it is not the rule of the Way to say 'to-morrōw' " (*Mathnawī* 1.132-3, cf. 111.2628 and note). Nicholson's note on 1.133 quotes from Farīdu'd Dīn 'Aṭṭār, *Tadhkiratu'l Awliyā* 2.179.10 "A thousand years multiplied by a thousand years to come are present (*naqd*) to thee in this 'Moment' (*waqt*) in which thou art"; and on 1. 1142-8 Wali Muḥammad's explanation that "the Ṣūfīs believe that at every moment a world (*'ālamī*) is annihilated and that instantaneously the like of it comes

[22] Cf. St. Augustine, "The world is pregnant with the causes of things as yet unborn" (*De Trin.* III. 9. 16).

[23] As in Sanskrit, *adṛṣṭa*.

into existence, because God has opposite attributes which never cease to be displayed; e.g. He is both Muhyī, 'the One who brings to life', and Mumīt, 'the One who puts to death[24]' ". So "this 'I-hood' comes to me from Him moment by moment" for so long as I live" (*Mathnawī* 1.2917): "every instant that Loved One assumes a new garment" (Shams-i-Tabrīz, *Dīwān*)[25].

The Ṣūfī, then is "'the son of the Moment'... the Ṣūfī's kind father, who is the 'Moment', does not let him be reduced to the necessity of looking to the morrow... He (the Ṣūfī) is of the River[26], not of time, for 'with God is neither morn nor eve': there the past and the and the future and time without beginning and time without end do not exist... He (the Ṣūfī) is the

---

[24] "The root of the mystery" of the only momentary reality of existences is referred to the opposite attributes also by Jāmī, *Lawā'ih* 26; these are respectively those of Mercy and Majesty (*jamāl* and *jalāl*) of which the reflections in this world man calls good and evil, existence and death. God is he "who killeth and maketh alive" (AV. 13. 3. 3; I Sam. 2. 6, 1 Kings 5. 7).

[25] For this origin of "I-hood" cf. ŚB. 7. 3. 2. 12 (see my "Sunkiss", JAOS. 60. 47); and for the "garments", BG. 2. 22, *Phaedo* 87 D, and Meister Eckhart, Pfeiffer p. 530 ("volgunge ist materie, daz diu sêle an sich nimet niuwe forme unde begît die sie vor hâte. Daz si ûz einer wandelt in die andern, daz ist ir tôt, under der si ûz gêt, der stirbet si, die si an sich nimet, dâ inne lebet sie").

[26] Here, of course, the "River" is *not* the "stream of time", but its source: "ein brunne in der gotheit, der an allen dingen ûz fliuzet in der êwikeit und in der zît" (Meister Eckhart, Pfeiffer p. 530).

son of that 'moment' by which is to be understood only a denial of the divisions of times, just as 'God is One' is to be understood only as a denial of duality, not as a description of the true nature of Unity" (*Mathnawī*, VI. 2715, Heading). Nicholson's Note points out that "River" here represents "the indivisible continuity of the spiritual world, where all things 'coexist in an eternal Now'"; also, on VI. 2782, that inasmuch as the uninterrupted coming and going of thoughts "never ceases for a single instant, they must be phenomenal manifestations of an Essence which alone is changeless and parmanent". Time, in other words, is an imitation of eternity, as becoming is of being, and as thinking is of knowing.

V

CHRISTIAN AND MODERN

In Christianity, the significance of the Present is asserted by the words of Christ, "Let the dead bury their dead" [1] and "Take no thought for the morrow" (Mat. 8. 22 and 6. 34). Aristotle's ἄτομος νῦν is unmistakeable in I Cor. 15. 51, 52 "Behold, I show you a mystery; We shall not all sleep, but we shall all be changed. In a moment, in the twinkling of an eye (ἐν ἀτόμῳ, ἐν ῥιπῇ ὀφθαλμοῦ), at the last trump ... the dead shall be raised incorruptible, and we shall be changed" [2]; a dictum that also reminds us of the Buddhist "Single-instant Awakening" (*eka-kṣaṇa-sambodhi*). For, again, just as for Aristotle and the Buddhists, corruptibility is inseparable from any existence in time; and to be "raised incorruptible" can only imply a passing over from the flux of temporal exist-

---

[1] Who are "the dead"? "Dead is the man of yesterday, for he has died into the man of today; and the man of today is dying into the man of to-morrow" (Plutarch, *Mor.* 392 D).

[2] This can be applied by no means only to the resurrection of the body in the distant future but (as in Islām) to the present moment of enlightenment, when "the soul which lay dead in a living body doth rise again" (St. Augustine, *Sermo* [*De scrip. N. T.*] 88, 3. 3), or as St. Thomas expresses it to "the first instant that grace inheres".

ence to a present eternity in which there is neither any yesterday nor a to-morrow, and in which the Christian has already lived in so far as he has been able to fulfil the commands of Christ to have done with the past and to take no thought for the morrow. I think it is in just this sense that A. A. Bowman observes that "the religious preoccupation with life is specifically the preoccupation with a life of experience which is momentarily reborn in every fleeting instant"[3]: and it would appear that the true Christian is really expected to be, and will be, as much as the Ṣūfī, a "son of the moment", and as much as the Buddhist Arahant a Freedman, "for whom there is neither past nor future" (S. 1.141)[4]. The reality of the eternal present is bound up also with that of the Holy Ghost, whose operation is immediate,—"And suddenly (*ἄφνω*) these came a sound from heaven as of a rushing mighty wind" (Acts 2. 2)[5].

---

[3] A. A. Bowman, *Studies in the Philosophy of Religion,* 1938, 2. 346. Cf. René Guénon "he who cannot escape from the standpoint of temporal succession is incapable of the least conception of the metaphysical order" (*La métaphysique orientale,* Paris 1939, p. 17).

[4] "Think on God and thou wilt find 'is' where 'has been' and 'shall be' cannot be" (St. Augustine, *In Joan. Evang.* 38. 10).

[5] Cf. Acts 22. 6 "Suddenly (*ἐξαίφνης*) there shone from heaven a great light", and II Cor. 6. 2 "Behold, now is the accepted time, behold, now is the day of salvation" (*ἰδοῦ, νῦν καιρὸς εὐπρόσδεκτος, ἰδοῦ νῦν ἡμέρα σωτηρίας*).

"Sudden" (*sub-it-aneus*) is literally "going stealthily"; and *ἄφνω* also has the meaning "mysteriously"; and we find these ideas also in India with reference to the divine procession and immanence, for example, in RV. 1. 145. 4 where Agni *sadyo*

In this connection St. Thomas, discussing the problem, Whether the Justification of the Ungodly Takes Place in an Instant or Successively (*Sum. Theol.* I-II. 113. 7) decides that such justification is "not successive, but *instantaneous*"[6] [i.e. just what the Buddhist would have called a "single-instant awakening"]; for such a justification depends upon the movement of Grace, which is sudden, and man's free-will "whose movement is by nature instantaneous"[7]; the justification cannot be successive, because "to will and not to will—the movements of the free-will—are not successive, but instantaneous"[8]. In answer to the further objection that opposite conditions cannot coincide in the same instant and so there must be a last instant in the state of sin

jātas tatsāra, for which Grassmann writes "kaum geboren schleicht" and one might say "like a thief in the night", or Muṇḍ. Up. 1. 1. 6 and 2. 2. 16, *adreśyam agrāhyam ... sūṣūkmam ... guhācara ... antaś carate bahudhā jāyamānaḥ,* as in Maitri Up. 2. 5 *sa va eṣa sūkṣmo'grāhy'dṛśyaḥ ... ihaivāvartate.*

Further, as to this speed: "Even now when I (God) am present here, I stand at the same time also there" (Philo, *Sacr.* 68); "it (νοῦς) has not moved as one moves from place to place, but it is there" (Hermes Trismegistos, 16. 2. 19); "the One, immobile, is swifter than the mind ... past others running, *this* goes standing" (Īśā Up. 4).

6 St. Thomas' "instant" is strictly atomic, and his argument rests upon the fact that such instants are not parts of time.

7 In the things above time no interval whatever divides cause from effect or beginning from end. It would be an interesting hermeneia—not, of course, an etymology—to connect "repentance" with *repente.*

8 "The journey of the spirit is unconditioned with respect to time and space" (Rūmī, *Mathnawī,* 3. 1980).

and another in the state of grace, he replies that "the succession of opposites in the same subject must be looked at differently in the things that are subject to time and in those that are above time. For in those that are in time, there is no 'last instant' in which the previous form inheres in the subject; but there is the last time, and the first instant that the subsequent form inheres in the matter or subject; and this for the reason, that in time we are not to consider one instant as immediately preceding another instant, since neither do instants succeed each other immediately in time, nor points in a line, as is proved [by Aristotle] in *Phys.* VI. 1. But time is *terminated* by an instant. Hence in the whole of the previous time wherein anything is moving towards its form, it is under the opposite form; but in the last instant of this time, which is [also] the first instant of the subsequent time, it has the form which is the term of the moment. But in those things that are above time it is otherwise... That which is justified is the human mind, and this is above time, though it is subject to time accidentally, in so far as it understands with continuity and time[9]... We must therefore... say that there is no last instant that sin inheres, but a last time; whereas there is a first instant

[9] In other words, aeviternal, like the angels or, as reason mortal, and as intellect immortal (though "reason" is sometimes used in the sense of "intellect", and had originally this higher meaning). On the "two minds" (mortal and immortal) cf. my "On Being in One's Right Mind" in *Review of Religion* 7, 1942, 32-40: "metanoia" is a change, i.e. transformation, of mind.

that grace inheres; and in all the time previous sin inhered".

All this might have been expressed, and perhaps even more clearly, in terms of the circle (ὁ τροχὸς τῆς γενέσεως, *bhava-cakra*) and its (seventh) ray; temporal succession corresponding to motion along its circumference and the *ex tempore* motion of free-will to centrifugal motion (fall or descent into matter) and centripetal motion (ascension or resurrection).

In the *Summa Contra Gentiles* I. 14, 15 St. Thomas discusses the eternity of God. He bases his argument on the assertions of God's *immutability* in Malach. 3. 6, Jac. 1. 17 and Num. 23. 19; he quotes Aristotle, "time is the enumeration of motion" (*Phys*. 11-5-219 B) and points out that only those things that are in time can be measured, but "God does not move at all, and so cannot be measured by time; neither does he exist 'before or after' or no longer exist after having existed, nor can any succession be found in Him... but has the whole of His existence at once (*simul*); and that is the nature (*ratio*) of eternity"; and he concludes with Ps. 101. 13 (102. 12) "But thou, O Lord, shalt endure for ever" and 28 (27) "But thou art the same, and thy years shall have no end".

In the *Summa Theologica* I. 10 "On the Immutability of God", St. Thomas distinguishes more fully between time, aeviternity, and eternity. "The idea of time consists in the numbering of before and after in movement; so likewise in the apprehension of the uniformity of what is outside movement, consists the idea of eternity. Further, those things are said to be measured by time which have a beginning and end in time... But as whatever is wholly immutable can have no succession, so it has no beginning and no end... Eternity is called 'whole', not because it has parts, but because it is wanting in nothing... the expression 'simultaneously whole' is used to remove the idea of time, and the word 'perfect' to exclude the *now of time*... The *now that stands still* is said to make eternity[10]... Aeviternity differs from time, and from eternity, as the mean between them both... The angels, who have an unchangeable being as regards their nature with changeableness as regards choice... are measured by aeviternity... Time has before and after; aeviternity in itself has neither before nor after, which can, however, be annexed to it; while eternity has neither before nor after, nor is it compatible with such at all. [But] aeviternity is sometimes taken for 'age', that is, a space of a thing's duration; and thus we say 'many aeviternities' when we mean 'ages'".

"Aeviternity", then, is the term that could be applied to the lifetime of the Indian Gods "born with a life (*āyus*, cf. *αἰών*)[11] of a 'thousand years'; even as one

[10] "The *now of time* is the same as regards its subject in the whole course of time, but it differs in aspect... as being here and there... Likewise the flow of the *now* as alternating in aspect, is time. But eternity remains the same according to both subject and aspect; and hence eternity is not the same as the *now of time*" (I. 10. 4 ad 2). This is, of course, Aristotelian, as well as according to Boethius.

[11] Etymologically cognate, both words can mean either "life" or "age". The IE root is *I*, to "go", (present also in *αἰών*, *ἀεί*, *aevum*, *aeternus*, ewig, ever and aye); in its fre-

might see in the distance the farther shore, even so did they behold the farther shore of their own life" (*Śatapatha Brāhmaṇa* 11. 1. 6. 15, cf. *Taittirīya Saṁhitā* 5. 7. 3f.); their "not dying" (*amṛtattva*) contrasting on the one hand with that of the man who lives for a hundred years, "not dying" prematurely, and on the other with the timeless immortality of Brahma.

Further (*Sum. Theol.* I. 10. 6), "time is one". Not because it is a number, "for time is not a number abstracted from the thing numbered, but existing in the thing numbered[12]; otherwise it would not be continuous; for ten ells of cloth are continuous not by reason of the number [ten], but by reason of the thing numbered". The position is quite Aristotelian; the piece of cloth does not stop being a piece of cloth at the end of each yard and then begin again; it is one piece of cloth; and so in the case of any extent, whether

---

quentative sense, that of continuation in a given state, it implies to "exist" or "be". When Agni is contrasted with the other Gods, as "the only immortal", he can be called *viśvāyus*, "the whole of life", and this totality is analogous to fulness of a man's "whole life" (*sarvam āyus*) who does not die before old age.

On *αἰών* as [like *āyus*] the complete period, either of each particular life or of all existence, v. Aristotle, *De Coelo* 1. 9. 15; on *αἰών* and *χρόνος* cf. Philo 1. 496, 619" (Liddell and Scott).

[12] This seems also to have been William of Ockham's view: "his main purpose in the Tractatus de successivis is to show that motion, place, and time are not entities separate from the respective realities, viz., the moved body, the located body, and the moved body in time. Ockham thinks this the true opinion of Aristotle" (P. Boehner, *The Tractatus de Successivis attributed to William of Ockham*, St. Bonaventura, N. Y., 1944, p. 30).

of time or space. *Time and space are continuous*. Both, like numerical unity, are infinitely divisible.

"Examine", St. Augustine says, "the mutations of things and thou wilt find everywhere 'has been' and 'will be'. Think on God and thou wilt find 'is' where 'has been' and 'will be' cannot be... Being is a term for immutability... There is primal and absolute life, in which it is not one thing to exist and another to be, but the same thing to be and to exist; and primal and absolute intelligence, in which it is not one thing to be living, another to understand, but to understand is to live, and is to be, and all things are one" (*In Joan. Evang*. 28, 10; *Sermo* 7.7; *De Trin*. 6.10.11). Again, in God, "nothing is past, as if it were no longer; nothing is future, as if it existed not yet. Whatever is there, simply *is*" (*In Ps*. 101, *Sermo* 2.10). And: "What is *the same*, save that which *is*? ... Nobody hath *the same* from himself... the body that he hath is not *the same*... Nor doth the human soul itself *stand*... Man's mind itself, which is called rational, is mutable, is not *the same*... 'But Thou art always the self-same' (Ps. 101.27f.)... Man in himself *is not*, for he is changed and altered if he does not participate in Him 'Who is the same'. He *is* when he sees God. He is when he sees Him WHO IS[13]; and by seeing Him WHO IS,

[13] "I am that I am" is the Greek version of what was really in Hebrew "I become what I become"; the Greek considering Him as "He is in Himself", the Hebrew as "He is turned toward us", becoming "the God of Isaac and the God of Jacob". Both concepts are common in the Vedic tradition; on the one hand, "HE IS, by that alone can He be apprehended"

he also begins, according to his measure, to be... But how? Through charity" (*In Ps.* 121)[14].

Perhaps even more striking in its wording: "Behold we speak and say 'in this year'... Say rather to-day, if you would speak of anything in the 'present... This, too, amend, and say 'in this hour'. But of 'this hour' what have you got? Some moments of it are already past, and those that future have still to come. Say 'in this moment'. But in *what* moment?... What then have we got of these 'years'?" (*In Ps.* 76. 8).

Time and eternity had been admirably discussed by Boethius, who is often cited by St. Thomas. To begin with, in *De Trin.* I. 4 he remarks that "God is 'ever' (*semper*) because 'ever' is with Him a term of present time, and there is this great difference between the 'now' which is our present, and [the 'now' which is] the divine present, that *our* 'now' connotes changing time and sempiternity; while God's 'now' abiding, unmoving, and self-subsistent makes eternity. Add *semper* to *aeternitas*, and you get the ever-flowing, incessant 'now' and therefore perpetual course of time that is

---

(KU. 6. 13), on the other "Thou, Agni, art Varuṇa at birth, and becomest (*bhavasi*) Mitra when kindled" (RV. 5. 3. 1) and "Became (*abhavat*) the Sun of men" (RV. 1. 146. 4, cf. John 1. 4).

[14] "Through charity"; for example, the practise of *maitrī, karuṇā, muditā, upekkhā* in the Buddhist *brahma-vihāras* (cf. in my *Figures of Speech or Figures of Thought*, pp. 147,148); for as Meister Eckhart says, "Alsô minnet got alle crêatûre gelîch und erfüllet sie mit sînem wesenne. Und alsô süllen wir mit minne fliezen ûf alle crêatûren. Des vindet man vil an den heidenen, daz sie zuo disem minnerîchen friden nâtiurlîcher bekenntnüsse kâmen" (Pfeiffer p. 273).

'sempiternity'"; and he doubts whether God's 'ever' is a form of time at all. In *De consol.* V. 6 he remarks that the common judgment of those who live by reason is that God is eternal (*aeternum*)[15] and so "let us consider what eternity is... It is the perfect possession of an interminable life *all at once* (*tota simul*)... whereas there is nothing placed in time which can embrace the whole of its life at once... For it is one thing to be led through an interminable life (which Plato attributed to the world)[16], and another thing to embrace the whole of an interminable life present in all its complexity". Of the transitory moments of time he says that in a way they imitate the now that stands still, so that at every moment a thing "seems to be". And so, "following Plato, let us call God 'eternal' and the world 'everlasting' (*perpetuum*)". Then he points out that God's "foreknowledge" [so called] ought rather to be called "the knowledge of a never fading instant than a *fore*knowledge, as if of the future. Wherefore it is not called a *pre*vision (*praevidentia*) or *fore*sight but rather an *on*sight (*provi-*

[15] In the Loeb edition, misrendered "everlasting". For Boethius, eternity is in-finite, i.e. without beginning or end, but not a duration, not "lasting"; it is time that "lasts".

[16] It does not seem necessary to discuss the problem of the "eternity of the world" in the present context. I will only observe that the Christian "world without end" seems to refer to the world in one sense (that in which time can be called "interminable"), and to *this* world in another sense (that in which a given time has a beginning and end). Just as in tradition, there are cycles that begin and end, but the series of of cycles has neither beginning nor end.

dentia)[17], because, placed far from lower things, it overlooketh all things, as it were, from the highest summit of things... and so not disturbing the quality of things which to Him are present, but in respect of time are future".

On this basis Boethius is able to deal effectively with the problem of free-will and "pre"-destination. For "God beholds those 'future' things which proceed from freewill, [not as future but] as present"; and freedom to will or nill is no more impugned by this present inspection or onsight than are the acts of a man in a distant field controlled by our looking on at what he is doing.

To understand this more fully it must be remembered that as Boethius has already said (V. 1) "freedom to will or nill" is the work of reason; while the so-called act of choice according to which we "do what we like" is not an exercise of freewill at all but an irrational and passive reaction to external stimuli; and that, as

---

17 Sanskrit *prajñā,* etymologically Greek *προνοία* and Latin *pro-gnosis,* is attributed to the all-seeing, omniscient Spiritual Sun and Self; it is a knowledge of all things, not derived from an observation of their occurence.

18 Both here in the sense of *νοῦς, intellectus vel spiritus,* as in St. Augustine *De ordine* 2. 50 "If reason is immortal... and if I am reason, then that by which I am called mortal is not mine"; not as reason is sometimes distinguished from intellect, as in Augustine *De Trin.* 15. 25 "the intellectual cognition of eternal things is one thing, the rational cognition of temporal things another" or as in Boethius *De consol.* 1. 6 where he speaks of himself as a "rational and mortal animal" and this means that he "has *forgotten what he is*".

St. Thomas says, the operation of reason or the mind (insofar as the latter really acts) is "above time". In discussing "fate", Boethius has already (IV. 6) compared time to the circumference of a circle of which the centre (*punctus medius*)[19] is eternity[20], and pointed out that "everything is by so much the freer from fate, the more it draws near to the pivot (*cardo*)[21] of all things; and if it clings fast to the firmity of the Supernal Mind, being free from motion, it also transcends the necessity of fate": that is, evades the causal efficacy of acts, which "take place" only in the world, *of* which the Freedman is no longer, though he may still be *in* it. In other words, the movements of free-will are real, but their occurrence is *ex tempore*[22]:

---

[19] Dante's "punta dello stelo a cui la prima rota va dintorno .... da quel punto depende il cielo, e tutta la natura" (*Paradiso* 13. 11, 28. 41); "apri gli occhi ... e vedrai il tuo credere" ... nel vero farsi come centro in tondo" (*ib.* 13. 49).

[20] "Ad id quod est quod gignitur, ad aeternitatem tempus, ad punctum medium circulus, ita est fati series mobilis ad providentiae stabilem simplicitatem".

[21] The *punctum medium*, referred to above as "indivisible", i.e. ἄτομος.

[22] Not in time; nor in eternity, but between them; for the motion must have ceased when its goal, the centre, has been reached; and so the motion will be, figuratively, spiral. Even the fallen angels could not have fallen for so long as they subsisted in the uncreated life; apart from a "creation", which necessarily involves some degree of "separation" from the centre, neither a Fall nor a Redemption are conceivable. These are the two "halves" of the cycle of existence; but in eternity extroversion and introversion coincide; and this actually guarantees the final apokatastasis of every "fallen spark".

and that they seem to us to be past or future is only the effect of our positions relative to the now of eternity.

Meister Eckhart: "God is creating the whole world now, this instant (*nû alzemâle*). Everything God made six thousand years ago and more when He made the world, God makes now instantly (*alzemâle*)... where time has never entered in, and no shape was ever seen ... To speak of the world as being made by God yesterday or tomorrow were a folly in us; He makes the world and all things in this present Now (*gegenwürtig nû*) ... what was a thousand years ago and what shall be a thousand years hence, all that is there in the present, —all that is overseas as much as what is here" (Pfeiffer pp. 190, 192, 207, 266, 297). Again, "in eternity, there is no before or after... To live in that eternity, so help us God!" (*ib.* 190, 192). In these words Meister Eckhart summarises as briefly as possible the doctrine of Time (time) and Eternity (Time) that we have already followed up through two millennia; and he states its significance for us,—"it is just for this that I was born" (*ib.* p. 284).

Again, "there is a power in the soul untouched by time... for God himself is in this power as in the eternal Now (*in dem ewigen nû*). Were the spirit always joined with God in this same power, a man could never age. For the Now in which God made the first man, and the Now in which the last man shall pass away, and the Now I speak in, all are the same in God in whom there is nothing but one Now... one and the same Eternity... Take the first brief words (of John 4. 23) *venit hora et nunc est.* He who would worship the Father [in spirit and in truth] must set him in Eternity with his longings and his hopes. There is one, the highest part of the soul, that stands above time and knows nought of time or body. All that happened a thousand years ago, the day that was a thousand years ago is in Eternity no farther off than the very hour I am in now; nor is the day to come a thousand or as many years hence as could be counted any farther off in Eternity than is this very hour that I am in" (Pfeiffer pp. 44, 45, 57).

So also when he speaks of the world as a "circle"[23], centred upon God, whose works are its circumference. "This is the circle that the soul runs round, all that the Holy Trinity hath ever wrought... and, as it says in the Book of Love, 'When I found it ever endless, then I cast myself into the centre of the round (*daz punt des zirkels*)... That point is the power of the Trinity, where it hath done all its work, itself unmoved. Therein the soul becomes omnipotent... therewith atoned (*geeiniget*) she is capable of all things... the essential point, where God is just as far from as he is near to all creatures[24]... there is she eternally insistent" (*êwiklîche dar bestêtiget wirt, ib.* pp. 503, 504).

[23] St. James' *ὁ τροχὸς τῆς γενέσεως*, and Indian *bhava-cakra;* the cycle of time. On the symbolism of the circle cf. Dionysius, *De div. nom.* 5. 6; St. Thomas Aquinas, *De principio scientiae Dei* 14; René Guénon, *Le symbolisme de la croix;* and my "Vedic Exemplarism" in *HJAS* I. 45.

[24] *Śatapatha Brāhmaṇa* 10. 5. 2. 17 "Both near and far away; for inasmuch as He is here on earth in the flesh He is near, and inasmuch as He is That One in yonder world He is also far away".

This is the point that St. Bonaventura speaks of when he compares God to a circle, of which the centre is everywhere (*Itin. mentis* 5); Dante's *punta,* a cui la prima rota va dintorno; and the *bindu* that marks the centre of every Indian *maṇḍala* and *yantra.*

And, further, as regards this Point, which is *the* Point of Time, "to know it we must be in it, beyond the mind and above our created being; in that Eternal Point where all our lines begin and end, that Point where they lose their name and all distinction, and become one with the Point itself, and that very One which the Point is, yet ever remain in themselves nought else but lines that come to an end" (Ruysbroeck, *De septem custodiis,* ch. 19).

All this symbolism is bound up with the doctrine that equates the persons of the "severalty of Gods" (Viśve Devāh i.e. the hierarchy of Angels, Intelligences or Powers), and likewise the Justified Deceased with the rays of the Intelligible Sun[25]: as, e.g. in RV. 1. 109. 7 "there be the very rays with which the Fathers of old were united", 10. 64. 13 "where we are met together at the Nave, Aditi confirms our kinship"; ŚB. 1. 9. 3. 10 "the rays of Him who glows yonder are the Perfected (*sukṛtaḥ*)[26], and what highest light there is[27], that is Prajāpati", and 2. 3. 1. 7 "the rays, indeed, are the Several Gods, and what highest light there is,

---

[25] "Not the sun whom all men see, but Him whom few know with the mind", AV. 10. 8. 14; for parallels, see *Psychiatry* 8, 1945, p. 288, Note 7.

[26] "As a Perfected (*sukṛta* = τέλεος) Self, I passed into the uncreated Brahma-world" (CU. 8. 13).

that is verily Prajāpati, or Indra"[27]; so that "under the theory of procession by powers, souls are described as rays" (Plotinus, *Enneads* 6.4.3), and "there shalt thou back into thy Centre fall, a conscious Ray of that eternal All" (*Manṭiqu'ṭ Ṭair*). It will be observed that these, together with the concept of "motion at will" (passing in and out) preclude any pantheistic interpretation on the heretical sense of the word[28]; were there no multiplicity in unity, to "pass in and out" would be meaningless; what the doctrine implies is a "fusion without confusion" or "distinction without difference" (*bhedābheda*), —one end of any ray is confused with its centre, the other distinct from it, and the Perfected are both.

Dante, when he is speaking of Eternity, makes many references to this "essential point" or "moment". All times are present to It (il punto a cui tutti li tempi son presenti, *Paradiso* 17.17); there every where and every when are focussed (dove s'appunta ogni *ubi* ed ogni *quando, ib.* 29.12). "The nature of the universe, such that it stills the centre and moves all the rest around, hence doth begin as from its turning-post" (*meta, ib.* 27.106)[29], and "from that point depend heaven and

[27] I.e. the Sun himself, represented by the solar disk, the Sun-door.

[28] In the proper sense, of course, a "pantheism" is inevitable; for if God be less than All, there will be something external to his essence, by which he will be, not infinite, but limited.

[29] In this metaphor of a chariot race, a "circus", I think *meta* is not literally the starting-point, but the post round which the turn is made.

all nature" (28. 41)[30]; It is a flaming point of light, and "round it there wheeled a circle of fire so rapidly it has surpassed the motion which doth swiftest gird the universe" (28. 25)[31], and this heaven "hath no other *where* than the divine mind" (27. 109)[31]; "there, perfect, ripe and whole is each desire; in it alone is every part there where it ever was, for it is not in space, nor hath it poles... whereby it thus doth steal it from thy sight" (22. 64). Also, he says, "neither before nor after was God's 'moving on the face of the waters'" (29. 20),—and, to cite Philo Judaeus, "there is an end, then, of the notion that the universe came into being 'in six days'" (LA. 1. 20): "every moment the world is renewed, life is ever arriving anew" (Rūmī, *Mathnawi* 1. 1142).

"Nor hath it poles", that is, contraries, or pairs of opposites; this is "the Paradise in which Thou, God, dwellest", of which the wall, as Nicolas of Cusa says, "is built of the contradictories"—of which the past and future are, from the present standpoint, the most significant pair, "veiling us from the vision of God", as Rūmī says—and whoever would enter in must first have overcome the highest Spirit of Reason that guards the strait gate that distinguishes them (*De vis. Dei* Ch. 9)[32]. These contraries, of which the extended world

[30] "Imperishable Brahma, flame, less than the least, wherein are set the worlds and all things in them" (Muṇḍ. Up. 2. 2. 2), "like a sparkling fiery wheel" (Maitri Up. 6. 24).

[31] It is only in this sense that God can be thought of as a "place": τόπος in Gnostic texts, *loka* in the Upaniṣads.

[32] The Logos: "I am the door, by me...".

is made, are the Symplegades, that must be passed by every traveller homeward bound. Moreover, Cusa says, "Whatever is seen by us in time, thou, Lord God, didst not *pre*-conceive, as it is. For in the eternity in which thou dost conceive [33], all temporal succession coincides in one and the same Eternal Now. So there is nothing past or future where past and future coincide in the present ... Thou indeed, my God, who art thyself Eternity absolutely, art, and speakest [thy Word] above the now and then" (*ib.* ch. 10). And so: "Draw me, O Lord, for none can reach thee save he be drawn by thee; free me from this world and join me (*jungar,* Skr. $\sqrt{}$*yuj*) unto thee, God absolutely, in the eternity of glorious life. Amen" (*ib.* ch. 25).

At this point it will be convenient to consider briefly the curious resistance that contemporary mentalities oppose to the concept of a static being definable only by negations of all limiting affirmations, all procedure from one experience to another. The most striking aspect of this resistance is the fact that it is almost always based on feelings: the question of the truth or falsity of a traditional doctrine is hardly ever raised, and all that seems to matter is whether one likes the doctrine or not. This is the sentimentality of those who would rather than arrive at any goal, keep on going not merely until it is reached, but "throughout all time", and who confuse their activity, which is only an un-

---

[33] Of this conception Meister Eckhart speaks elsewhere as "the act of fecundation latent in eternity". It coincides with the eternal birth of the Word "by whom all things were made".

finished procedure from potentiality to act, with a *being* in act.

Thus R. A. Nicholson protests that "to our minds the atoms, which have extension neither in space nor in time, seem insubstantial enough" (*Studies in Islamic Mysticism,* 1921, p. 154). The objection may be with special reference to the Ash'arite atoms as constituents of real magnitudes, but applies as well to the unique Atomic Time or Now of Eternity that we have been considering". As W. H. Sheldon remarks, "men *feel* that what cannot be put in terms of time is meaningless": but, he continues, "the notion of a static, immutable being ought to be understood rather as signifying a process so intensely vivacious, in terms of time as extremely swift, so as to comprise beginning and end at one stroke" (*Modern Schoolman* 21. 133). We cannot and may not, in fact, ignore that these who speak of a static, immutable, and timeless being above the partiality of time, also speak of it as an immediately beatific experience and possession of all things that have ever been or shall ever come into being in time; not to mention the realisation of other possibilities that are not possibilities of manifestation in time; it is a more and not a less "life" that subsists in the "naught" that embraces all things, but is "none" of them. In the same way men recoil from Nirvāṇa (literally, "despiration"), although it pertains to the definition of Nirvāṇa to say that "he who finds it, finds all" (*sabbam etena labbhati,* KhP. 8) and that it is the "supreme beatitude" (*paramaṁ sukham, Nikāyas, passim*)!

"Eternal time" (Time, as distinct from the time that flies), as Boethius says, "is the total and perfect possession of interminable life in its simultaneity". The answer to what men "feel" when they shrink from "eternity", just as they shrink from the "self-naughting" that shocks them only because they have not, in themselves, distinguished between the Self that "never became anyone" from the inconstant Ego of "this man, so and so", is to be found in such words as those of Meister Eckhart: "to have all that has being and is lustily to be desired and brings delight; to have it simultaneously and partless (*zemâle ungeteilet*) in the soul entire and that in God, revealed in its unveiled perfection, where first it burgeons forth [34] and in the ground of its essence, and all there grasped where God grasps himself,—that is happiness. And yet another

[34] *In dem êrsten ûzbruche:* so, neither yet displayed (future) nor still hidden (past), but unmanifest-manifest (*vyaktāvyakta*). On this state of perfect promise and eternal bloom, the state of highest tension conceivable, which is also the paradigm of an ideal art, see my "Theory and Practise of Art in India", *Technical Studies* 3, 1934, p. 75. This perfect moment occurs at "Dawn", cf. Mayūra's *Sūryaśataka* 26 "Rather, at the time of beginning, when the splendour of the Sun, like a painter's brush uncloses, as it were [an opening eye or flower] the whole world picture". It is like the archer's stance at the moment of release, when the arrow is on the point of leaving; and as in Chinese art "the movement represented is the pause before the action begins when the body is [still] tense" (H. Fernal in the *Burlington Magazine*, Jan. 1936, p. 26). It is remarkable that the Shakers also held that that beauty is best which is "peculiar to the flower", not that "which belongs to the ripened fruit".

Fulness of Time: if someone had the art and the power to gather up the time and all that ever happened in six thousand years or that shall be until the end of the world[35], all this assembled in one present Now (*ein gegenwertic nû*), that would be the 'Fulness of Time'. That is the Now of Eternity (*daz nû der êwikeit*), when the soul knows all things as they are in God, as new and fresh and lovely, as I find them now" (Pfeiffer p. 105).

Such is the Fulness, from which, as the Upanishad puts it, "if Fulness be taken, Fulness still remains" (BU. 5. 1). No Ṣūfi, no one in *samādhi*[36], no Western mystic, *raptus,* ever felt diminished by his "moment of illumination". To see "the world in a grain of sand, and eternity in an hour"—if one only could—for whom would it not be enough? Freedom to be as and where and when one will, or everywhere, or nowhere—does such a liberty as this imply a privation only because the word *in*-dependent states a positive good in the negative terms of a freedom from all limitations, the existence of which is inseparable from any form of existence in time and space? How can one "feel" that there must be something wanting in an "eternity" that by definition "wants for nothing"? In this "all-obtaining" (*sarvāpti*) [37] there remain no desires whatever un-

---

[35] I.e. throughout all time, in the then generally accepted sense: but rather, as a Hindu might express it, throughout all times, of which the present world-age is only one. It would have been the same for Origen.

[36] Literally and etymologically, "synthesis".

[37] "The Spirit of Life (*prāṇa*) is the Prognostic Self (*prajñ-*

satisfied; nor can one imagine a being "without desire" otherwise than when all desires are satisfied, desire then being at rest in its object. It is a matter of experience for those who speak of it so certainly, and those who live as they lived will see what they saw; but for others, is such an experience one to be shunned, or one to be desired?[38]

Here, because "all change is a dying", as Plato (*Euthydemus* 283 D, cf. *Parmenides* 163 A, B), Meister Eckhart, and our whole tradition recognize, every meeting is a meeting for the first time, and every parting is for ever. Meetings and partings (of which birth and death are but special cases) are only possible in time, and they please or grieve us only because "we" are or, rather, mistakenly identify ourselves with, the mutable psycho-physical tabernacles that our Self assumes, and so think of ourselves as creatures of time. It is

---

ātman), Life and Immortality together... Whoever approaches Me as Life and Immortality, he lives out his life in this world, and obtains inexhaustible (*akṣiti*) immortality in the world of heavenly-light... This is the 'All-obtaining' in the Spirit of Life" (Kauṣ. Up. 3. 2. 3).

[38] I am aware that there are modern men for whom the satisfaction of all possible desires would not suffice; beyond that, they want to entertain and to pursue others not yet satisfied. These are those who have never known what it means to be *contented* with a little, and cannot imagine a state of contentment even though possessed of everything there is to be desired; men "who would not like to live without hunger and thirst if they could not also *suffer* the natural consequences of these passions" (Plato, *Philebus* 54 E); men who forget that nothing *more* can be added to infinity.

as creatures of time that the fading of flowers and the death of friends distresses us. There are such and such desires or loves (*kāmāḥ*) that men feel: and these "are real (or true), but overlaid by falsity (or unreality)... For, indeed, whoever of one's loves deceases, one no more gets a sight of *here*. But those who are still alive here, and those deceased, and whatever else one wishes for but does not get, all this he finds who enters in *there*" (Chāndogya Up. 8. 2. 1, 2). This does not mean that "here" and "there" are simply here and now on the one hand, and there and hereafter (post mortem) on the other; for the universe itself, "all beings and all these desires *are* content (*samāhitāḥ*)[39] in this 'City of God' [the living body], in the ether of the heart[40]. But what is left over (*atiśiṣyate*)[41] of the 'city' when age overtakes it and it breaks up?[42] What is left over

[39] *Samāhita*, "in *samādhi*": literally and etymologically, "synthesised".

[40] "The kingdom of heaven is within you".

[41] The same question is asked in Kaṭha Up. 4. 3, 5. 4, and answered, "That", i.e. Brahma, God. If St. Paul could say, "I live, yet not *I*, but Christ in me", what would have been "left over" when this man Paul died? "The body of man is subject to overmastering death, but the image of Eternity (*αἰῶνος εἴδωλον*) *remaineth* (*λείπεται* = *atiśiṣyate*) alive" Pindar, *Dirge* 131. "It is in the soul of man, that is, the rational or intellectual soul, that we must find that image of the Creator which is immortally planted in its immortality... And this image of God... when, finally, it shall altogether adhere to Him... will be 'one spirit' [I Cor. 6. 17]... then, it will live immutably" (St. Augustine, *De Trin.*).

[42] "For here we have no continuing city, but we seek one to come" (Hebr. 13. 14).

of it is the true (or real) 'City of God'[43],—the sorrowless, ageless, deathless Self (*ātman*) [44] whose desire is true (or real), whose concepts are real [45].... Those who fare away having already found (or known) here the Self and those true desires (or loves), they become 'movers-at-will' in every world" (*ib.* 8. 1. 1-6) [46]. And this concept of the "two cities" and of true and false desires is Augustinian, but before him, Platonic; for

[43] "Two loves have created these two cities ... the earthly ... and the heavenly ... Wherefore let every man question himself as to what he loveth; and he shall find of which he is a citizen" (St. Augustine, *De civ. Dei* 14. 28 and *In Ps.* 64. 2); and "right is he who should grieve without a limit, who, for the love of what endureth not, eternally doth strip him of this love, the love that breathes aright" (*Paradiso* 15. 10-13 + 2).

[44] "the self-subsistent, undesirous, youthful Self, unaging and undying, whom if one knows, he fears not death" (Atharva Veda 10. 8. 440). For the "City of God" (*brahmapura*, see *ib.* 10. 2. 28-33).

[45] The last words, descriptive of the Self, are repeated and further expanded in Maitri Up. 7. 7.

"The objects of earthly loves are mortal, hurtful and loves of shadows that change and pass, for these are not what we really love, not the good that we are really in search of. But there is the true object of our love, where we can be with it, grasp it and really possess, where no covering of flesh excludes", Plotinus, *Enneads* 6. 9. 9.

[46] I.e. "shall pass in and out, and find pasture" (John 10. 9); Taitt. Up. 3. 10. 5 "up and down these worlds, eating what he will and assuming what aspect he will"; RV. 1. 113. 9 "where there is motion at will"; *Cloud of Unknowing*, ch. 59 "so subtle in body and in soul together, that we shall be then swiftly where us list bodily, as we be now in our thought ghostly".

"there are false pleasures in the souls of men, imitations or caricatures of the true pleasures" (*Philebus* 40 C); of which the false pleasures (*ψευδεῖς ἡδοναί*) are affects, mixed with pain, and the true (*ἀληθεῖς*)[47] those that are taken in beauty, primarily as exhibited in mathematical forms, and those of learning[48], in which there is no admixture of pain (*ib.* 51). In other words, Augustine's, while we are thinking of eternal things, the things that do not change, we are participating in eternity. Eternity is not far away from us, but nearer than time, of which both parts are really far away, one far ahead of us and the other far behind us; whatever *is* true, however, was always true and will be true for ever. "Truth", alike in Brahmanism, Buddhism, Islam and Christianity is as much as Eternity one of the

---

[47] *Ὁ γε τὸ ὂν λέγων καὶ τὰ ὄντα τἀληθῆ λέγει*, *Euthydemus* 284 A; Verum mihi videtur id quod est, St. Augustine, *Soliloq.* lib. 2, c. 5, n. 8. But the truth of facts and the truth of principles pertain to different levels of reference. Skr. *satyam* (√*as*, to "be"), "truth" or "reality" can likewise be predicated either relatively of temporalia or absolutely of immutable being. For a fuller discussion see above, pp. 2, and 25, n. 6.

[48] Not, of course, a mere erudition, but "the learning that draws the soul away from becoming to being", knowledge of the "essence that is for ever, and is not made to wander between generation and destruction" (Plato, *Republic* 485 B, 521 D): "all true knowledge is concerned with what is colourless, formless, and intangible... not such knowledge as has a beginning and varies as it is associated with one or another of the things that we now call 'realities', but that which is really real" (*Phaedrus* 247), "really real" corresponding to *satyasya satyam, paramārtha-satyam,* ens realissimum, *τὸ ὄντως ὄν*.

names of God, and it is only our forgetfulness that makes us need to pray "O thou who changest not, abide with me", as a Ṣūfī might desire to make his *waqt, ḥāl.* If the eternal basis of existence—*dhamma*—is both here and now (*diṭṭhe dhamme*) and timeless (*akāliko*), it might be well to see what it "feels" like here and now, before "feeling" so much afraid of it. If, indeed, we do not participate in eternity *now,* perhaps we never shall [49]

There is also another way in which the nature of the experience of eternity can be suggested. It can be assumed that a given mind cannot think of more than one thing at a time. But this does not mean that the life of the intellect is only arithmetical. Even the giving of names to things, an intellectual power, is the endowment of many successive events with a kind of permanent identity, even though a pseudo-identity, apart from time; without this, the communication of feelings would be possible, but not a communication of thoughts; and this already indicates that the intelligible world has more to do with eternity than with time. And in the same way spatially, consider the complexity of the art in the artist, that is to say, of the form in the artist's mind, where although it is there one, this one form is the form of many things that could be and will be afterwards thought of separately. For example, in thinking of a "house", one also thinks of many other things, at least of a floor, walls, and roof. A more complex example is afforded by the well-known, although far

---

[49] BU. 1. 4. 15, 4. 4. 14; CU. 7. 25. 2, 8. 1. 6; BG. 18. 58.

from unique, instance of Mozart, who heard his compositions first not phrase by phrase, but as a *totum simul,* and thought this "actual hearing of the whole together" better than the subsequent hearing of the whole extended. The most complex example is that of Dante's vision of "the universal form" of the world picture [50] of which he says that "within its depths I saw interned, bound up by love into one volume [51], all the scattered leaves of the whole world, substances and accidents and their successions, as it were together (*insieme*) [52] fused in such a way that what I speak of is one simple flame ... Such at that light doth man

[50] Plato's "eternal paradigm" on which the sensible world is modelled, *Timaeus,* 29: "the world-picture (*jagac-citra*) painted by the Spirit (the Self of all beings) on the canvas of the Spirit, and in which it takes a great delight" (Śaṅkarācārya, *Svātmanirūpaṇa* 95),—just as for Empedocles (Diels fr. 23) and for Plato (*Timaeus* 55 C) the Creator paints, and in Islam is called a painter (*muṣawwir,* qur'ān 53. 24) or, to employ Philo's equivalent, just as the ideal pattern of the thing that is to be is as it were "engraved" on the maker's mind (*Opif.* 16-22).

[51] Cf. Empedocles (Diels fr. 26) "all brought together in one order by Love".

[52] *Insieme,* "in-same", as regards both time and place. "The centre of the whirl, wherein all things come together, so as to be one only" (Empedocles, Diels fr. 35, 36): "all are the same there and nevertheless distinct; in the same way that the soul possesses the knowledge of many things without confusion, each fulfilling its own task when the need arises" just as in the case of the "powers" that inhere in a seed (Plotinus. *Enneads* 6. 9. 6): "Nû sint alliu dinc gelîch in gote unde sint got selber" (Meister Eckhart, Pfeiffer p. 311). One might say, plures, non tamen multa, sed unum.

become that to turn thence to any other sight never could he by any possibility consent!" (*Paradiso* 33. 85-100). One thinks also of the immediate operation of "mathematical genius"; and of a Buddha's vision that "does not work in terms of the composites" but alights where he wishes, "'just as one might skip the sequence of a text', coming to the point at once" (Vism. 411). There is also the mystery of the possibility of the communication of ideas from one apparently circumscribed mind to another, hardly understandable unless on the assumption of some transcendent element common to both [53]. And, finally, there is the fact that is "a single knowledge of contrary things", of which the intellect can be aware at the same time, when, for example, it entertains the idea of "temperature", in which the notions of hot and cold are included [54]; from which an inkling can be had of what it might mean to be "liberated from the pairs of opposites", for example, from a knowledge only in terms of the past and

[53] "All human properties proceed from One ... otherwise one man could not understand another in the sound" (Jacob Boehme, *Sig. Rer.* 1. 2). "In all conversations between two persons tacit reference is made to a common nature. That third party, or common nature, is not social, it is impersonal; it is God" (Emerson, *Varieties of Religious Experience*): "Self [of the self], who controls the speech from within ... the un-understood Understander" (BU. 3. 8. 17, 23). "Consciousness is a singular of which the plural is unknown" (Erwin Schrödinger, *What is Life?* 1945, p. 90). More generally, W. M. Urban, *The Intelligible World* (1929) and *Language and Reality* (1939).

[54] Cf. St. Thomas Aquinas, *Sum. Theol.* 1. 75. 6, where this supplies an argument for the incorruptibility (immortality) of the *anima intellectiva*.

future that, as we have seen, "are a veil to thee from God". And though omniscience may be nothing quantitative, and not a mere aggregate of knowledges of things, it still holds good that the synoptic and synthetic powers of the merely human intellect provide us with an analogy of what it might be like to see and know all things at once, not in contradistinction of subject and object, but where "to know and to be are the same thing"[55]. One does not imagine that the

[55] This was not, as is generally supposed, first enunciated by Parmenides, fr. 5. His τὰ γὰρ αὐτὸ νοεῖν ἔστιν τε καὶ εἶναι simply means that "that which can be thought is the same as that which can be" (see Burnet, *Early Greek Philosophy*, 4th ed. 1930, p. 173, n. 2). Plotinus, *Enneads*, 5. 9. 6 quotes Parmenides' words, but although by this time it was possible for the infinitive to be the subject of a sentence and, in fact, Plotinus uses τὸ εἶναι as subject (*Enneads* 3. 7. 6), his citation of Parmenides' words is to show that "*in the immaterial* knowledge and the known are the same", and while this implies that *there* the knower, knowledge, and the known are the same, what is actually predicated is hardly more than the Scholastic *adequatio rei et intellectus*,—Plato's "making that in us which thinks like unto the objects of its thought", which, *if* they be eternal and divine, will restore our being to its "original nature" (*Timaeus* 90). It seems to have been St. Augustine who first explicitly enunciated that *in divinis* to live, to know, and to be are one and the same thing (*De Trin.* 6. 10. 11, *In Joan. Evang.* 99. 4, and *Conf.* 13. 11). To be what one knows is not a given status, but one to be achieved. What is presently true is that "as one's thinking is, such he *becomes*" (*yac cittas tanmayo bhavati)*; and it is because of this that thinking should be purified and transformed, for were it as centred upon God as it now is on things sensibly perceptible, "Who would not be liberated from his bondage?" (Maitri Up. 6. 34. 4, 6).

Divine intellect is a sort of dictionary, but much rather a Word or a Form that is the form of many different things, to use the language of exemplarism [56].

In conclusion, although much could be added to what has already been said [57], I shall only trace the persist-

---

[56] Cf. my "Vedic Exemplarism, *HJAS* 1, 1936, 44-64. The Angels, as Meister Eckhart says, have fewer ideas and use less means than men. God has only one idea and is but that one, and needs no means at all.

[57] I have made only a limited use of F. H. Brabant's admirable and comprehensive *Time and Eternity in Christian Thought,* 1937. G. E. Mueller's "Experimental and Existential Time" (*Philosophy and Phenomenological Research,* 6, 1946, 424-435) deals with Greek and Christian sources. I do not understand his words, "Over against this absolute affirmation of being in the recurrences of natural time lies the Hindu negation of time"; for it is hardly a "negation of time" to say that "time and the timeless" are *both* forms of God, who is similarly "*both* formed and formless, "audible and silent" and so on, and it is certainly as true of India as of Greece that "the beauty and substance of human culture is made manifest in the seasonal celebrations and festivals of the year of the soul". There is a valuable discussion of our subject by Alberto Rougés, in his *Las Jerarquías del Ser y la Eternidad,* Tucumán, Argentina, 1943. Alexander's *Space, Time, and Deity* I have not seen. Joseph Katz in his "Eternity—Shadow of Time" (*Review of Religion* 11, 1946, 36-45) tries to invert the Platonic and traditional concept of time as being an image or imitation of eternity, and also makes the very common mistake of supposing that because the satisfaction of all desires is only possible "beyond time" such a satisfaction must be "postponed", forgetting that the *nunc aeternitatis* is as present here and *now* as it ever was or will be; actually, it is the secular utopiast, who believes in the perfectibility of human society, that postpones his felicity, while the *Sūfī* "son of the moment" "takes the

ence of the traditional concept of time and eternity in some of the English metaphysical poets. For example, Herrick:

O yeares! and Age! Farewell,
Behold I go,
Where I do know
Infinitie to dwell

And there mine eyes shall see
All times, how they
Are lost i'th'Sea [58]
Of Vast Eternitie

---

cash and lets the credit go". Katz, moreover, thinks that the satisfaction of all desires would be "meaningless" because the needs that prompted them would be lacking; Traherne supplies the answer,—admitting that "no joy could ever be were there no want", he says of God that "He infinitely wanteth all His joys ... and all those wanted pleasures He infinitely hath ... His life in wants and joys is infinite, And both are felt as His Supreme Delight"!

[58] On the "everlasting day", see above, p. 13. Cf. also Meister Eckhart's "Plunge in, this is the drowning". It should be needless to say that "drowning", "anonymity", "becoming no one" are of two utterly different kinds, according to whether it is into the upper or the nether waters that one plunges. One shrinks from the upper waters only because because of attachment to the empirical and transient Ego that "is not my Self"; one should shrink from a drowning in the nether waters, for this implies the loss *even* of one's individuality, so that one has no longer, properly speaking, a name, but only a number, like a convict, or as in proletarian societies, becomes a statistical unit and no longer a person. To have "lost one's self" in the infinite, and to have lost one's self in the in-

Where never Moone shall sway
The Starres; but she,
And Night, shall be
Drown'd in one endless Day.

Herrick's second verse combines the thought of Joshua Sylvester's

To-day, To-morrow, Yesterday
With Thee are one, and instant aye,

and Angelus Silesius:

Wenn du das Tröpflein im grosse Meere nennen,
Denn wirstdu meine Seel' im grossen Gott erkennen[59].

and also Labadie's beautiful last testament,

"I surrender my soul heartily to God, giving it back like a drop of water to its source, and rest confident in him, praying God, my origin and ocean, that he will take me into himself and engulf me eternally in the abyss of his being"[60].

This well-known motif—"the dewdrop slips into the shining sea"—has, like the analogous concept of the sparks of the divine fire that arise from and return to it, and like that of the exile returning home, a long παράδοσις,

---

determinate are, literally, worlds apart, as, far apart as heaven from hell. "When shall I come to be again in Varuna?" RV. 7. 86. 2.

[59] Angelus Silesius, *Cherubinische Wandersmann* 2. 25.

[60] Quoted by Dean Inge, *Philosophy of Plotinus,* 2nd ed. 1. 121.

traceable through Ruysbroeck [61], Meister Eckhart [62] and Dante [63] to Greek sources in the West, and in the East to the Ṣūfis, notably Shams-i Tabrīz [64] and Rūmī [65], and to Buddhist [66], Vedic [67], and also Chinese [68] sources. For example, in the *Praśna Upaniṣad* 6.5 (of which a Buddhist version in the *Aṅguttara Nikāya* 4.198 is an almost literal equivalent) we find:

"Just as the flowing streams that move towards the sea, on reaching it, are coming home, their name-and-shape are broken down, and one speaks only of the 'Sea', even so of this Witness (*paridraṣṭṛ*) [69] the six-

---

61 See below. Ruysbroeck makes constant use of the term "immersion", an exact equivalent of Pali *ogadha,* in the common expression *amat'ogadha* "immersion in, or plunge into, the Undying", thought of as an "unfathomable sea".

62 "As the drop becomes the ocean, so the soul is deified, losing her name and work, but not her essence", Pfeiffer p. 314.

63 "Nostre pace, è quel mare, al qual tutto si move", *Paradiso* 3.85, 86.

64 "Enter that Ocean, that your drop may become a Sea that is a hundred 'seas of 'Omān'", *Dīwān* (Nicholson, Ode XII).

65 *Mathnawi* 4.2616 and passim.

66 A. 4.202; Udāna 55; M. 1.487.

67 Chāndogya Up. 8.10.1, Muṇḍ. Up. 3.2.8, and Prasna Up. 6.5. Cf. RV. 7.86.2 "When shall we come to be again in Varuṇa?" (the Sea) = Brahma "whose world is the Waters", Kauṣ. Up. 1.7.

68 *Tao Te Ching* 32 "To Tao all under heaven will come, as streams and torrents flow into a great river or sea". In the present work I have only neglected Chinese sources for want of sufficient knowledge of them.

69 The "Witness" and the "Person" are one and the same, but respectively as seen *sub specie temporis* and *sub specie aeternitatis.*

teen parts (*kalā*) that move towards the Person (*puruṣa*) [69], when they reach the Person, are coming home, their name-and-shape are broken down, and one speaks only of the 'Person'. He (who is a Comprehensor) then becomes without parts (*akalā*), immortal... 'On whom the parts are supported, as spokes are set in the

---

"Witness (*upadraṣṭṛ*), yea-sayer, support, experient, Great Lord, and also the Self Supreme, such is the Highest Person called when in this body" (*Bhagavad Gītā* 13. 22); "the experient, immanent Person" (Maitri Up. 6. 10). This is "he who looked forth through beings" (Kaṭha Up. 4. 6); the "unseen Seer (*draṣṭṛ*) ... other than whom there is none that sees" (Bṛhadāraṇyaka Up. 3. 8. 11). This Person is also Agni as *upadraṣṭṛ*, Jaiminīya Brāhmaṇa 3. 261, in whose likeness the Purohita functions as the king's charioteer and *upadraṣṭṛ* to see that the latter does no wrong, *ib.* 3. 94. So, then, the Witness is our "inner Man"; from whom nothing done by the "outer man" is hidden. Again, "the Person here, the Comprehensor, is himself that Progenitor (Prajāpati) who is the Year whose fifteen parts are his properties, the sixteenth part, that which abides (*kṣīyate*, *κτίζω*); which abiding part, compared to the nave of a wheel, is represented by the new-moon night about which the half-months of waxing and waning revolve (Bṛhadāraṇyaka Up. 1. 5. 14, 15); it is with this residual (*atisiṣṭā*) sixteenth part, when the other parts have been mortified, that one understands the Vedas (Chāndogya Up. 6. 7). This is the residual "Person" whose unity (*ekatvam*) is reached by transcending all his aspects (Maitri Up. 4. 6), and beyond whom there is nothing more whatever (Kaṭha Up. 3. 11). This is also the Residuum (*ucchiṣṭam*) that the Atharva Veda, 11. 7, describes as the "synthesis (*samādhi*) of all things" and "origin of all"; this is the Fons Vitae, and I know of no other text in which the fulness of the *content* of Eternity is so adequately expanded.

hub of a wheel, him do I know as the Person to-be-known,—let not death disturb you!"

As one last illustration of the universality of the ideas that have been discussed above I cite from John of Ruysbroeck's *Sparkling Stone* (ch. 9): "For it we possess God in the immersion of love—that is, if we are lost to ourselves—God is our own and we are his own: and we sink ourselves eternally and irretrievably in our one possession which is God... And this down-sinking is like a river, which without pause or turning back ever pours into the sea; since this is its proper resting place". And from *The Book of Truth* (ch. 10): "And this takes place beyond time; that is, without before or after, in an Eternal Now... the home and the beginning of all life and all becoming. And so all creatures are therein, beyond themselves, one Being and one Life with God, as in their eternal origin".

We have traced, according to ability, the history of the meanings of the concepts of time and of eternity: the one, in which all things come and go, and the other, in which all stand immutable. We can only accept these established meanings without question, if the integrity of communication is to be preserved; except for those who elect to live in a merely existential world without meaning, they have always been, and will always remain an integral part of human experience. For "non-spacial and non-temporal intuition is the condition of the interpretation of the space-time world itself"[70] "all states of being, seen in principle, are simultaneous

[70] Wilbur M. Urban, *The Intelligible World,* 1929, p. 280.

in the eternal now ... (and) he who cannot escape from the standpoint of temporal succession so as to see all things in their simultaneity is incapable of the least conception of the metaphysical order"[71]; and in the "unified experience of reality the whole process of creation from the Primal Covenant to the Resurrection is a single timeless moment of Divine self-manifestation"[72].

OṀ NAMO ANANTAYA KALANTAKĀYA!

---

[71] René Guénon, *La métaphysique orientale*, pp. 15, 17.

[72] R. A. Nicholson, Commentary on Rumī, *Mathnawī*, I. 2110-2111.

Printed and bound by CPI Group (UK) Ltd, Croydon, CR0 4YY

29/04/2025

14663997-0003